Making Intimate Connections

Are you looking for a Rebuilding seminar near you?
Do you lead Rebuilding seminars for others?
You'll find seminar information online at
www. rebuilding.org. Dozens of locations in the US,
Canada, and Europe.

RebuildingBooks
For Divorce and Beyond

MAKING INTIMATE CONNECTIONS

7 Guidelines
for
Great Relationships
and
Better Communication

Dr. Albert Ellis
& Ted Crawford

Impact Publishers,® Inc.
ATASCADERO, CALIFORNIA

ATTENTION ORGANIZATIONS AND CORPORATIONS:
This book is available at quantity discounts on bulk purchases for educational, business, or sales promotional use. For further information, please contact Impact Publishers, P.O. Box 6016, Atascadero, CA 93423-6016, Phone: 1-800-246-7228. E-mail: sales@impactpublishers.com

Library of Congress Cataloging-in-Publication Data

Ellis, Albert
    Making intimate connections : seven guidelines for great relation-
ships and better couple communication / Albert Ellis, Ted Crawford.
        p. cm.
    Includes bibliographical references and index.
    ISBN 1-886230-33-1
        1. Rational-emotive psychotherapy. 2. Marital psychotherapy. 3.
Interpersonal relations. I. Crawford, Ted. II. Title.

RC489.R3 E4438 2000
616.89'156--dc21   00-058065

Publisher's Note
This publication is designed to provide accurate and authoritative information in regard to the subject matter covered. It is sold with the understanding that the publisher is not engaged in rendering psychological, legal, or other professional services. If expert assistance or counseling is needed, the services of a competent professional should be sought.

Second Printing, August, 2001

Impact Publishers and colophon are registered trademarks of Impact Publishers, Inc.

Cover design by John Magee, San Luis Obispo, California.
Printed in the United States of America on acid-free paper,
Published by ***Impact*** 🅢 ***Publishers®, Inc.***
POST OFFICE BOX 6016
ATASCADERO, CALIFORNIA 93423-6016
www.impactpublishers.com

Dedication

This book is dedicated to my spouse, Janet L. Wolfe, who has nicely used REBT to gracefully put up with me for thirty-five years.

— Albert Ellis

With thanks to Alfred Korzybski, Albert Ellis, Lynn Hamilton and my wife Jolanta Crawford.

— Ted Crawford

Acknowledgements

To Emmett Velten and Kevin Fitz-Maurice, who read the manuscript of this book and gave very helpful comments.
— Albert Ellis

To all those who made it easy for me to learn what would work. And to all those others who made it difficult for me because they helped me fine tune my understanding and skills.
— Ted Crawford

Contents

Chemistry, Connections, and Communication

The ABCs of Self-Disturbance

J ay was a chemistry whiz. A university professor and a genuine expert in his field, he could discuss it in exacting detail with his students, his colleagues, and his wife, Marjorie. Expressing his feelings, however, was another matter altogether. After all, feelings are far less concrete than chemical formulas! One of the major reasons Jay married Marjorie was that she expressed her feelings so beautifully; he found he only had to agree or disagree with her; he needn't give her detailed descriptions of his own feelings. So he got by quite well — for a while.

Marjorie eventually tired of his constant, "Yes, I feel that way, too," and wanted him to be more specific. Jay had no clue what to say to her — and then beat himself mercilessly for being so uncommunicative. "Marge is right. I *should* feel as she does. And even if don't, I *must* express whatever feelings I do have, otherwise she'll see what a zombie I am!" Jay's demands on himself — that he *had to* have exciting feelings and that he *must* express them well — blocked him from saying almost anything and overwhelmed him with self-defeating feelings — great anxiety.

On her side, Marjorie first made herself angry with her own demands: "After all, I'm not asking very much from Jay and he simply refuses to talk to me about anything except chemistry problems. Who cares about that! Since I'm asking so little, he *should* try much harder!" Marjorie also brought on self-pity with: "After all I've done for him! I've really gone out of my way and poured my guts out to help him express himself — and now I get nothing, absolutely nothing. Poor me! Look how I'm cheated. How awful!"

Responding to Marjorie's anger and self-pity, Jay then made himself guilty: "She's rightly angry at me, and I *shouldn't* be causing her such grief! I'm really a rotten person for plaguing Marge like this! Not just inadequate; really *rotten!*"

And the cycle continued: seeing how badly Jay kept downing himself, Marjorie made herself guilty: "Here he is having such a hard time communicating his feelings and instead of showing him some pity, I'm childishly pitying myself and enraging myself against him, as I *shouldn't*. A fine wife I am!"

Typically, as in so many marriages where communication breaks down, Jay and Marjorie strongly "shoulded" on themselves and each other, thus creating and escalating a vicious cycle of self-downing, anger, and self-pity. As you can readily imagine, their communication kept going downhill.

~ ~ ~

Our goal in this book is to give you the tools you need to deal with hassles like Jay and Marjorie's. You'll learn how to avoid communication traps, and how to get out of them if and when they snare you. Our approach to couples communication is based on *Rational Emotive Behavior Therapy*, a system Al** developed in the mid-1950s and which is now one of the most highly regarded and widely used therapeutic methods worldwide.

Al started the whole thing, and he tells the story this way:**
When I created Rational Emotive Behavior Therapy (REBT) in January 1955, I had one main idea: To help my clients make themselves happier and more self-fulfilled.

This was an old plan of mine, which I started devising in my teens, when I was pretty disturbed myself. I had severe phobias — particularly of speaking in public and talking to strangers — so I haunted the bookshelves of several New York public libraries to find out how I could be less neurotic and much happier. I pored over the writings of the ancient philosophers — Confucius, Lao-Tzu, Gautama Buddha, Epicurus, Epictetus, and Marcus Aurelius — and used much of their material successfully on myself. Eureka!

** *Throughout this book, we have identified ourselves to you this way: "Al" or "[AE]" is Albert Ellis; "Ted" or "[TC]" is Ted Crawford.*

I got completely over my fear of public speaking and became phenomenally good at it. As for talking to strangers — particularly attractive young women — I made myself into one of the best pick-up artists in the city. I kept reading and writing on human happiness even before I became a psychologist, and wrote what I thought was a great book, *The Art of Never Making Yourself Unhappy*. Although I failed to convince a publisher that it would make the best-seller list, I did use some of its ideas, and stubbornly refused to make myself miserable about my "great lost opportunity."

In 1943, when I was thirty, I became a practicing psychologist and changed my goal from helping people become *happy* to helping them become *less emotionally disturbed*. I discovered that the vast majority of my clients were so busy tying themselves up in emotional knots that they rarely enjoyed or actualized themselves — as they presumably were trying to do. So the goals of Rational Emotive Behavior Therapy had become, first, to help people conquer their emotional problems, and then to show them how to make themselves happier. Fulfilling both of these goals requires good communication with oneself and others. *To be less disturbed on your own, watch your self-communication. To relate well with other people, listen to your communication with them. Yes, both!*

I didn't fully realize when I started practicing REBT that it largely involves talking to others as well as to yourself. Like most other therapies, REBT is highly interpersonal. It focuses on your listening to and relating to a therapist, and on the therapist listening to, understanding, and creating an accepting relationship with you. REBT also shows you how to effectively deal with significant others — including those who could very well use therapy themselves! [AE]

Self-Communication

REBT, more than other therapies, stresses self-communication. The "ABCs" of emotional disturbance — a core concept in REBT — focus on what Al originally called the *self-talk* that people use to disturb themselves. These ABCs show how you hold conversations in your own head, and how you actually *construct* and *create* most of your self-defeating thoughts, feelings, and actions, and, therefore, you can also *deconstruct* and *reduce* them. The ABCs of Rational Emotive Behavior Therapy explain how you talk to yourself and others, and how using the ABCs helps you relate better.

As we begin our exploration of intimate communication, let's briefly outline these ABCs.

- REBT assumes that you, like just about all humans, have several basic *goals* or *values*, especially:
- to stay alive.
- to be happy when you are alone.
- to communicate with and have good relationships with a number of other people.
- to relate intimately with a few select people.
- to acquire useful information and education.
- to support yourself in some steady — and preferably enjoyable — vocation or career.
- to enjoy some kinds of recreational interests, ranging from games and sports to arts and sciences.
- to largely control your own life and not be too restricted by others, external conditions, or your own personal handicaps.
- to maintain and/or deepen an intimate relationship.

Deepen Your Relationship

For our purposes in this book we shall focus on the specific Goal: *to maintain and/or deepen an intimate relationship.* With this goal you will likely encounter both practical problems and emotional problems. The *Seven Guidelines* we present in this book are a set of attitudes and methods for dealing with both the practical and emotional problems of communicating with a partner.

If this is your main Goal, and you merely *want, wish,* or *prefer* to achieve it, you will usually feel contented or happy when you do, and sad, sorry, disappointed, regretful, or displeased when you don't. These negative feelings are "healthy" or "helpful," even though they are painful, because they push you to reduce the roadblocks to your Goal and to survive happily. This statement applies to any goals you may have.

Fine. So you look for happiness and avoid roadblocks. You figure out ways to solve life's difficulties, predict that you can do good problem-solving, and acquire a sense of what Stanford psychologist Albert Bandura calls *self-efficacy.* "I know how to do well and enjoy myself. Great!" Al calls this achievement-confidence (you can read more about it in his book, *Reason and Emotion in Psychotherapy,* revised 1994). It's a good place to begin our discussion of the ABC framework of REBT.

Goal — "I want to succeed in my relationship with John."
- *A (Activating Event)* — "John seems to like me and to want to be with me."
- *B (Belief)* — "Good! I like that! It means that I can probably relate well to other people I enjoy."
- *C (Consequences)* — Feeling of self-efficacy, achievement-confidence, self-mastery.

Why do you have "Beliefs" about achieving and about failing at your goals? Because that's "human nature." In order to survive and be happy, you practically always have to think about, evaluate, and rate your *Beliefs* and the *Activating Events* in your life to determine how to deal with them. So do other animals, but as a human, you have more complex beliefs. You react to Activating Events [A's] with feelings and actions, not just because they occur, but also as a result of your Beliefs [B's]. You do so *because* you are human. REBT assumes that your Consequences, (C's), follow from both "A" and "B," not one or the other.

When I first started to do REBT formally in 1955, I saw that it greatly helped individuals in talking to themselves and others. If you really understand how your Beliefs help or block you, and how you can change and control them, you can communicate much better. Also, you can help others, yourself, and your relationships considerably if you see how disturbed other people's Beliefs and Consequences are, if you unconditionally accept them despite their disturbances, and if you show them, using REBT, how to become less upset.

I saw this in the 1960's, but Ted in some ways saw it even more clearly than I. As he read REBT books and articles, he worked with scores of people, mainly on their communication problems. Although he had no graduate training in psychology or sociology, he soon became, in my opinion, one of the world's leading authorities on effective communicating. Ted created an unusual method for people listening and talking to each other called Revolving Discussion Sequence (RDS), and he also invented a number of other methods of interpersonal listening, some of which we shall later describe in this book. Although some of his methods may appear to be influenced by the work of Carl Rogers on active listening and unconditional positive regard, Ted has always said that he was mainly inspired by my early works on REBT. I am, of course, very pleased about this; we have been in close touch since

1962, and have collaborated by mail, phone, recordings, and personal meetings for more than 38 years.

Ted and I started to write this book in the 1960s, but both of our very busy lives got in the way. We didn't blame ourselves and we didn't make ourselves frantic, but continued to develop our REBT-oriented views on talking to oneself and others, and to experiment with these with groups, workshops, in our individual counseling, and in our own personal relationships. We now have much to write about — in fact, perhaps too much for one volume. Therefore, in this first volume, we shall not present all of our ideas, but mainly those that are related to REBT. [AE]

Rational Emotive Behavior Therapy sees all humans — yes, including you — as born-and-bred internal and external communicators. You obviously converse with others, usually in speech, and also with pictures, images, symbols, plays, films, gestures, grunts, laughter, and other kinds of signs. You also communicate with yourself, again, largely with talk and sentences, but also with meanings, philosophies, visualizations, symbols, formulas, dreams, art, music, and other kinds of expressions. In this book we shall mainly show you how to talk more effectively to yourself and others, because self-talk and speech are — for most of us — our most common means of communication. But behind these open discussions you also have many unspoken, implied, or unconscious ideas with which we shall also deal. Whether or not you are fully aware of doing so, you "speak" to yourself and to others in many implicit as well as explicit ways."

Communication Styles

Let's look at your internal and external communication styles to see how you can better understand and improve your own thoughts, feelings, actions, and how you can relate better to both yourself and others. In an era when the human race has had remarkable success in overcoming many diseases and afflictions, harnessing natural resources to produce vast amounts of food and power, and enormously improving world communication, we have hardly achieved peace and cooperation among our scores of nations and billions of people.

Rational Emotive Behavior Therapy originally assumed that you feel disturbed Consequences (C's) because you rehearse

Irrational Beliefs (IB's) — IB's you mainly learned from your parents and culture. Then you foolishly keep re-indoctrinating yourself with these harmful ideas. This is partly true. But after years of clinical practice and many research studies, REBT now recognizes that all of us are born with a tendency to take our strong preferences — both learned and innate — and *raise them* to unrealistic commands: "Because I *greatly desire* success and approval, I *must have* them!"

In any event, once you either adopt or construct *dire necessities* out of your strong preferences, you are in trouble. Because, obviously, other people and the universe rarely care whether your godlike demands are fulfilled. Worse yet, you, others, and external conditions frequently block your achievement of these demands. Tough!

If you, like millions of intelligent people, refuse to accept this reality, you may seriously depress yourself when life (e.g., you, other people, and conditions) doesn't turn out the way you think it *should*. Even when you do succeed, and when people and conditions actually treat you as well as you think they always "must," you may still panic and depress yourself. How do you know that the goals you demand and achieve today will *continue* to turn out well tomorrow? You don't!

You can easily adopt or create scores of helpful *Rational Beliefs*, (RB's), about unfortunate Activating Events, (A's), that occur in your life. They are almost always preferences, such as, "Even though I hate failing at an important goal or being rejected by a person whom I like, I can still lead a fairly happy existence."

Three Types of Irrational Beliefs

You can easily adopt or create many Irrational Beliefs, (IB's), about adverse Activating Events (A's), that plague you. You do this with unrealistic, illogical, and self-defeating *demands, commands, shoulds, oughts,* and *musts,* especially like these three:

1. "I, (ego), *absolutely* must perform well at important tasks and be approved by significant others. If I don't do well and get approval, as I *must,* I am a pretty *worthless person* who will *continually* fail and who hardly deserves good things in life!" This dogmatic demand often leads you to feel anxious, depressed, self-hating, and avoiding "risky" projects and relationships.

2. "You, (other people), who are involved with me absolutely must treat me kindly, lovingly, and fairly. If you don't, you are no good and should be damned and punished!" This grandiose demand frequently leads you to feel rage, fury, vindictiveness, and to create fights, feuds — and even wars — with others.

3. "The conditions under which I live, (my environment), absolutely must be comfortable and easy, must quickly and painlessly provide me with what I really want, and must not make me uncomfortable. If conditions are not this way, it's awful, I can't stand it, and life is hardly worth living or trying to make better!" This Irrational Belief often leads to feelings of frustration (particularly for those with low frustration tolerance (LFT)), discomfort, disturbance, anger, depression, and/or self-pity. It also tends to create laziness, procrastination, denial, rationalizing, and addiction.

To sum up: Irrational Beliefs, (IB's), may be grouped around the three major headings of *self, others,* and *conditions:*

1. I must always do well

2. Others must always treat me kindly and fairly

3. Conditions must always provide me what I want, the way I want it

Unless you are perfect and really do run the universe, take care! *Grandiose demands* and *commands* can sabotage many of your healthy goals, interests, and desires. Not every time — but often enough!

This goes as well for your efforts to communicate well with others. Your *preferences* to relate to them and have them carefully listen to you are fine. Your *desires* to induce them to agree with and to stop opposing you are usually sensible and sane. Your *wishes* to be fully understood are normally healthy and rational. Your *wanting* to be appreciated by them is understandable. So far, great!

Here's where lots of us get into trouble. Arrant *demands* that you *have to be heard* and agreed with are far from helpful; in fact, they're often unrealistic and cannot be fulfilled. Rather than helping you to communicate well with others, such demands can block closeness.

This does not mean that without absolutist *musts, shoulds,* and *oughts* you will automatically and easily become a peaceful, friendly, marvelous relater. Most probably you won't. As we shall show, you also require more than this. But giving up your godlike demands on yourself, on others, and on external conditions will help. Appreciably!

REBT and Communication with Others

This book will not solve most of the existing worldwide problems. Hardly! It will not eliminate dictatorships, wars, crime, homicide, ecological pollution, overpopulation, terrorism, political corruption, and other serious social evils. Not exactly! But if you use its principles and methods to communicate better with yourself and others, you will likely live more peacefully and enjoyably. Also, while using REBT ideas yourself — and, we hope, *communicating* them to others — you may improve your own and some other people's lives. From that not-so-small beginning, you may promote an eventual upswing of human cooperation.

We make no promises; but that is our hope.

2

The Challenge
of Accepting Reality

I s this just another self-help book that, once again, will show you how to stop upsetting yourself about anything and everything? No! Al has written several books like that, and this is not just one more. Yes, it uses and teaches you some of the main elements of Cognitive Behavior Therapy (CBT) and Rational Emotive Behavior Therapy (REBT), but it particularly focuses on your intimate relationships. What's new is that this book describes and tells you how to use the *Seven Guidelines For Great Relationships*.

"I Loved Mickey": Ted's REBT Tale

The *Guidelines* were born when Ted first learned Al's Rational Emotive Behavior Therapy in the 1960s and applied REBT to his life-long interest in improving interpersonal communication.

I especially applied REBT to communicating with Mickey, with whom I was madly in love.

Mickey, alas, had decided she didn't want anything to do with me. Her commandments of "no dates, no phoning, no visiting" seemed to leave me with no solutions — I was stuck! I felt hurt, devastated, and depressed, and, I thought, I *must* have great communication with Mickey; I don't have what I *must* have! Or so I believed. I had trouble sleeping, pushing myself past my tiredness, getting out of bed, going to work. Mickey's rejection left me emotionally wounded.

In Al's writing on Rational Emotive Behavior Therapy I noted his distinction between "wanting" and "needing." My problem was my mistaken belief that "I *must* have what I *want*." I decided to use the REBT distinction and to test what happened.

At that time in my life I had my own business selling eggs. I decided to practice making the REBT distinction between *wanting* and *needing* while going on regular sales trips. I pretended that each customer was Mickey, and while waiting for her to come to the door I silently said to myself, "Mickey I *want* to communicate with you, but I don't *have* to do so." *Have to, ought to, must, should, necessity,* and *need* are all interchangeable with each other. I had many customers so, in the course of a day, got lots of practice!

Sometime late one afternoon I heard someone singing, but didn't see anyone. I felt surprised to discover that I was singing, and felt euphoric and no longer tired. Now, seeing that I no longer *needed* what I *wanted* with Mickey, I wondered what I might do about getting the communication that I still desired.

What changed here? Certainly not Mickey, nor her forbidding me to see her. I wasn't communicating with her at all. The only thing that changed was my *Beliefs* — beliefs I hadn't even been aware of. I no longer believed that I *must* have communication with Mickey. I did not really *need* what I merely *wanted*.

Consequently, I was no longer wounded by her rejection. I could sing and be happy without her — even though I still loved her.

That was when my creativity kicked in. For the first time I realized that Mickey had not forbidden letters. I schemed about how to write notes that would interest and not offend her. First, I would not request anything — especially not communication.

Second, I would share what I was doing, feeling, or thinking. Third, I would write only on subjects that I thought would interest her. And fourth, I would write only in the present tense without reference to the past or future. I did this for a little over a year without hearing anything back. Finally I received a surprise post card inviting me to meet with her! We've been communicating ever since. [TC]

Distinguish Between Wanting And Needing

The Rational Emotive Behavior Therapy (REBT) distinction between *wanting* and *needing* is important and basic. When you don't *need* what you want, you are more honest with yourself and with other people.

Your Belief that you *must have* what you want tends to lead to self-deception and irresponsibility, and your so-called "need" justifies your acting demandingly. Also, when you don't get what you believe that you *must have* or *need*, you probably experience feelings of inadequacy, depression, hurt, and anger. You think it is *awful* to fail, and you judge yourself as a total failure. Confusing wanting and needing stops you from distinguishing between what you want and your demanding *shoulds, musts,* and *have to's.* Life is more fun, flexible, and creative when you let go of your *shoulds, musts,* and *needs.*

When I used REBT on myself, I decided that Al was right about the connection between thinking and feeling. They are two sides of the same coin: change my thinking and I change my feeling; change my feeling and I change my thinking.

I continued to explore Rational Emotive Behavior Therapy and its links to communication. I learned that most relationship problems stem from the failure to successfully share differences and disagreements, and that people mistakenly believe that such successful sharing is not possible.

Years later, when Jolanta and I met, both of us had been previously married and were now divorced. This time — for a change! — we chose to succeed. We talked over what we might do to achieve success, and developed the *Seven Guidelines* as the foundation for our upcoming marriage. Some of our friends were so impressed with how we used them that they started using the Seven Guidelines in their own marriages. You will meet Frank, an engineer and professor, who used them with his wife, Frances, and Michelle who used them with her fiancé — now husband — Hunter. [TC]

The Seven Guidelines

Guideline 1: Accept your partner "as is."
Guideline 2: Express appreciation frequently.
Guideline 3: Communicate from integrity.
Guideline 4: Share and explore differences with your partner.
Guideline 5: Support your partner's goals.
Guideline 6: Give your partner the right to be wrong.
Guideline 7: Reconsider your wants as goals.

Frank's Letter

Frank started with Guideline 1 and got up to Guideline 4 when he decided to share his experiences and success in using the Guidelines.

Did the Seven Guidelines change my life? Enormously! Initially, I simply found them puzzling and useless. But I persisted, and after a long time, I got into them — and they got into me. What a radical change!

I take the first Guideline to mean acceptance of *all things* as they are — not just Frances "as is." That was tough to see and the most difficult to apply. All my life I thought things *had* to be a certain way, otherwise they were not acceptable. What trouble that caused! Stubbornly I clung to the notion that things *must* be the way I think they *should* be.

Ted kept telling me otherwise, but I "stuck to my stuckness," until one day it hit me like a lighting bolt. I thought, why *should* things be as I insist? If the sky is blue, and I think it *should* be green, does that make sense? Of course not. It made no sense to refuse to accept what clearly "is." Yes, I may *prefer* it to be different, but *demand*?

Alas, I still did demand — and almost abandoned Guideline 1. The trouble was that while trying to apply this Guideline to Frances, I was not applying it to myself. I at first thought, "I *must* do it right every time, otherwise I'm a failure." Then I applied Rational Emotional Behavior Therapy to myself and said, "Well, I failed this time, but I am not a failure, not if I accept myself 'as is.' Let me start all over." So, just like Popeye, "I am what I *am!*" This is not to say I want to stay that way, but unless I see what I am and accept myself "as is," I wouldn't be able to change because I wouldn't know what I am changing from.

As I began to accept myself "as is," I also started to apply the Guidelines to my relationship with Frances. Like most other things in my life, I did not accept her as she was. I demanded that she be as I thought she *should* be. Naturally, I got nowhere. I decided to try Guideline 1 with Frances. Even when I failed, I did not give up.

Initially, Frances did not think I could keep Guideline 1 going. "He'll soon give it up." Slowly, she tested my determination. As I persisted with accepting her "as is" she was very impressed and she became more open to my ideas.

The other Guidelines were also very useful. Guideline 4 — to share differences to achieve a win-win outcome — stood out just like the first guideline. At first, I thought Frances ought to be a certain way that she was not. Following Guideline 1, I accepted Frances the way she was, and I still loved her. Then, before giving her my opinion on an important matter, I listened to her view, restated it until she agreed that I really understood it, and only *then* sometimes differed with her. When I listened to her view, and understood it to her satisfaction, she was much more open to hear my view and give it serious consideration. We often would move closer to each other's view.

I also invented a "playing it over" game for her to use with me. I told Frances, "If at any time you feel hurt by something I say or do, you can ask me to say it (or do it) over again and not hurt you this time." When she did so, I had up to fifteen minutes to re-collect myself (i.e., swallow my pride), and repeat the discussion in a manner she would find acceptable. Initially I needed to use the entire fifteen-minute waiting period. Now I am so used to this "game," I am willing to get into the matter right away. First, I need to know what *exactly* hurts her feelings. I listen carefully, then repeat what I think she is saying until she is satisfied that I understand her view. Since it is my intention to be nice to her because I love her very much, I find it easy to say it right the second time. I can hardly recall a single time when this approach did not work for us.

Success with the Guidelines came in making small changes in the way I saw things, but the effects of these changes were very pronounced. My life has become much more peaceful. This is an upward-spiraling phenomenon. Success encouraged me to apply the Guidelines more, and now I use them almost as a matter of habit, especially with people close to me. Other times, I may have to think first, then apply the Guidelines. [Frank]

～ ～ ～

Perfection Is Not Required

Most people react to these Guidelines with, "These are fine, but difficult." If they think in terms of trying to use them perfectly, they are right; our relationship guidelines *are* difficult to follow. However, if you think of them as *guidelines* — not as *commands* —

you can easily start to apply them and improve your communication and your relationship with your partner. We do not know anyone who uses them perfectly, including us.

The Guidelines you may have most difficulty with are #1, Accepting your partner "as is"; #4, Successfully sharing differences to achieve a win-win outcome; and #7, Changing your *want* into a *goal*. Let's take a look.

We (Ted and Al) agree that the very first Guideline will be the most difficult. One of the main principles of REBT, and which practically the whole human race has difficulty seeing and using, is called "acceptance." REBT teaches people that to be emotionally secure they need to *fully accept* three major human conditions:

1. You are fallible, and you'll often act inefficiently, badly, and even immorally. Too bad, but you will. Therefore, to avoid putting yourself down, and thereby *adding* to your fallibility, unconditionally accept yourself with this fallibility. Unconditional Self-Acceptance, (USA), is a central theme of REBT — and of many mental health programs.

2. Everyone else, including your partner, is also very fallible, and if you are wise you will give them Unconditional Other Acceptance, (UOA), in spite of their warts and failings. By all means accept them, as Guideline 1 states, "as is." Keep in mind, as we sometimes say to "perfectionistic" clients, "There's no reason any one *perfect* would want to be with you."

3. Conditions of living — your environment, ecology, economics, politics — are far from perfect and can create innumerable problems for you, your partner, and others. Tough! You don't have to like them. Hate them, if you will, and fight them. But accept conditions that you can't presently change — yes, accept — without unduly upsetting yourself and making the situation worse.

Two for the Road

So says REBT about acceptance. Jack and Jessamine loved each other intensely, but fought like hell almost every weekend when they were constantly together. Jack refused to accept himself "as is," with his small income as an erratically employed musician, his inability to play the violin perfectly, and his feeling of depression over his "great inadequacies."

Jessamine couldn't understand Jack's self-downing, because she thought he was wonderfully talented and the nicest person she had ever met. She violently opposed his self-denigration, but in doing so she helped him flagellate himself even more. He couldn't, he thought, please her — as he *absolutely must* — which made him more severely depressed.

Both Jack and Jessamine were terribly depressed about the lack of opportunities in the music industry, their financial difficulties, and the decrepit condition of their apartment building in a deteriorating neighborhood. They wanted to sell their condo and move to better quarters, but the state of their building and their own personal finances stopped them from doing so.

Al notes that when he saw Jack and Jessamine for marriage counseling, though Jack and Jessamine were intelligent and educated people, who quickly saw the REBT principles of acceptance and agreed that they would benefit from following them, they strangely clung to their demands. Jack *had to* do much better to accept himself with his (highly exaggerated) inadequacies. Jessamine periodically raved against Jack's "idiotic" self-downing. They collaborated, cursing the "stupid" and "impossible" building and the music industry. Jack became more depressed; Jessamine grew angrier. Both elevated their whining and low frustration tolerance. They seemed ready to throw in the towel on themselves, each other, and the world.

It took several months of REBT work — instead of the hoped-for several weeks — to convince Jessamine first, then Jack a little later, that their "as is" situations were bad, *very bad*, but still not *awful* and *hopeless.* Jessamine made a real effort to fully accept Jack with his self-downing and depression, no matter how "idiotic" she thought these traits were. In so doing, she helped him see that these traits were indeed bad, but that *he* was a worthy, lovable person. She also realized that putting him down for his behavior was helping to make him feel more inept and hate himself for "making" her so angry. She entirely stopped criticizing him and emphasized only his good traits, particularly his niceness. Jack was so amazed at her turnaround in accepting him "as is" that he worked harder than ever — with lots of encouragement from Jessamine and Al — to do so himself, and was largely able to succeed. He especially stopped blaming himself for being depressed, and as a result, has been much less depressed.

At the same time, both Jack and Jessamine worked on accepting the grim economic facts of their lives "as is." They firmly decided that things should be rotten when they are rotten and can't, at the moment, be changed. Then they were able to figure out some inexpensive things to do on weekends, such as joining a hiking group. These new activities kept them away from their deteriorating apartment house situation, interrupted their fighting, and proved to be thoroughly enjoyable. With their self-imposed emotional problems lessened, they were able to enjoy each other immensely once again.

Your views of yourself, others, and your life circumstances are not "all in your head," but your self-defeating beliefs about them are, and you can do something about those. In the next chapter we will look more closely at the challenge of accepting yourself, your partner, and your reality "as is."

3

Challenging Your "Shoulds" and "Musts"

"Can you give us an example of good communication that works if we use a Rational Emotive Behavior Therapy (REBT) approach and use the Seven Guidelines for Great Relationships?"

Yes, we can. Here's a true story. Ted was having dinner at the home of Mr. and Mrs. Jones. This amazing couple shared a disagreement they had with each other. Mrs. Jones vigorously presented her *husband's* side of their difference as if it were her own side.

"Then Mr. Jones presented his *wife's* side with the enthusiasm I would have expected him to use for his own side. To my great surprise, they both greatly enjoyed discovering and openly discussing a real disagreement that they had not yet resolved. They relished their difference! [TC]

Mr. and Mrs. Jones seemed to have figured out naturally how to use Guideline 4, "Share differences to achieve a win-win outcome," and Guideline 5, "Support your partner's purposes and goals." Most couples, however, do not naturally and easily do this, but can be shown the virtues of doing so and taught how to do it.

Winning With Thelma And Sol

Consider, for example, Thelma and Sol, two of Al's clients who came for REBT help precisely because they were both great arguers. They liked to show each other why their purposes and goals were absolutely right. Both enjoyed winning the argument and getting their way. Like many couples who come for marital counseling, they kept enjoying the battle — and losing the war. They particularly enjoyed fighting over the right ways to raise their son, Jim, and their daughter, Mona, and inconsistently won or lost these fights — as, of course, did their confused kids.

It was difficult convincing Thelma and Sol of the first three communication Guidelines, because they were reluctant to accept their partner "as is," and refused to stop trying to prove that they alone were truly *right*. They had even more difficulty seeing the virtues of Guidelines 4 and 5. They both wanted to gain a clear-cut *I-win-you-lose* position. Here is Al's comment:

I first helped them see that neither of them could consistently win, as both were good arguers and would rather die than lose. At best, therefore, they would be inconsistent parents, and that would do their children little good.

Moreover, they had to win the arguments to "prove" how bright and "worthwhile" they were. So when they didn't win, they felt worthless as parents and as persons; when they temporarily seemed to win an argument, they were afraid that they would lose *next time*. As a result, they were continually anxious, and there was no real win for either of them.

When I presented this to Thelma and Sol, they realized that the joy of winning an argument was wiped out by potential future self-downing, and that the temporary ego inflation led to later self-castigation and anxiety. Thus they — and their children — were actually losing even as one of them was "winning."

I pointed out that the best way to really win was to respect and appreciate the other's good arguments and thus achieve a win-win situation for both of them. As homework, they were persuaded to support each other's arguments for several weeks — quite a novelty to them! But they steadfastly tried to do so, and actually began to enjoy supporting each other's disagreements. Soon they were disagreeing less and agreeing more. Thelma, Sol, and their children were immensely pleased. [AE]

The Shoulds and Musts of Frank and Frances

Remember Frank and Frances in the last chapter? Let's look at their *musts* and see how their demands made them miserable before they began using the *Seven Guidelines*. Frances enjoyed long conversations on the phone with her friends and her mother. Frank, however, made himself furious about Frances "wasting" time on the phone because he insisted that she take care of the house and serve him, as a good wife *should*. He always had things for her to do.

When Frances was on the phone, he demanded, "How long will you be?" She usually replied, "Ten minutes," and Frank would begin to time her. After exactly ten minutes he would scream, "Your time's up! Get off the phone!"

Frances tried to bargain with Frank by saying, "I'm almost finished. I'll be off in another five minutes." He would reluctantly agree, but this time he'd stay in the room. Frances would then exclaim, "When you hang over me, you make me nervous. Please leave." He didn't leave and they argued while Frances was still on the phone. By the time she hung up, she was crying, and felt hurt and angry that he had "humiliated" her. His anger turned into rage.

Using REBT we can figure out Frank and Frances's powerful *absolute shoulds, needs, oughts,* and *have to's:*

Frances's Absolute Shoulds & Musts

1. Frank *must* give me "freedom." I *should* have control of my own life. I deserve, and *must* get, better care than I'm getting.
2. Frank *should* respect me!
3. I can't stand it! I *must* have the freedom to be myself. I must *not* remain with Frank!
4. If Frank leaves me, I'll be alone as I *must not* be. So I cannot, *must not,* leave him, because I cannot survive without him.
5. Frank *must not* act the way he does. He's a monster as he *must not* be.

Frank's Absolute Shoulds & Musts

1. I *must* have control of Frances and my marriage. I deserve, and *must* get, better care than I'm getting.
2. Frances *should* respect me!
3. I must *not* lose Frances. I *have to* intimidate her to *guarantee* that she will stay with me. She *must* obey me, like a good wife *should*!
4. Frances *must not* leave me alone to take care of myself, for that would be awful! Since she always comes back that proves my intimidation works. So to keep her I *must* continue to intimidate her. I can't stand giving in to her.
5. Frances *must not* act the way she does, and is an uncaring and unworthy wife as she *must not* be.

6. I *need* a good solution to this problem and Frank *absolutely should* arrange it! I *shouldn't* have to deal with such a bad situation. If he would behave better, as he *should*, he would do things my way.

6. I *need* a good solution to this problem and Frances *should* arrange it! I *shouldn't* have to deal with such a bad situation and if she would behave better, as she *should*, she would do things my way.

Let's briefly look at the above *shoulds* and *musts*. First, notice that each of the above *shoulds* and *musts* includes an unmet *want*. Both Frank and Frances are *rational* in that they *prefer* their partner to act differently.

Second, each of their *shoulds* and *musts* contradicts Frank's and Frances's own "reality." By using *shoulds* and *musts*, they hold that their situations *should not* and *must not* be the way they indisputably are. To each of their *preferences* they add *demands*. They mistakenly see their preferences and their demands as the same thing: "Because I *want* it so intensely, it *must be* the way I want it!"

Third, each one of Frank's and Frances's *shoulds* and *musts* is a grandiose, godlike *demand*, to which the other *should* and *must* magically cater.

If you're like most people, you're probably not completely satisfied with the way the world runs. And, if you believe in God, your absolutistic *shoulds* and *musts* are probably telling God that He or She acted wrongly. You tell God how the universe *should be* arranged: it *must* give you exactly what *you* want! Your will, not God's will, *should* be done! Even if you are not religious, you may be making grandiose demands that what you want *shall* be.

You may also use other words to express your absolutistic *shoulds*, *musts*, and *demands*. These other words include *have to*, *ought to*, *need*, and *necessity*. In "reality," you do not absolutely *need* anything, except in the conditional sense of "if." *If* you are going to drive your car, then you *need* gasoline or diesel fuel (unless you drive a solar-powered electric car!). You don't *absolutely need* to live, but if you *want* to live, you actually *have to* do a few things, such as eat and breathe. It is highly likely that you will die at some time, no matter what you do. So conditional *shoulds* and *musts* are often sensible and realistic, but absolutistic *musts*, such as, "No matter what, I *absolutely must* have a fine car," are not. "Under all conditions and at all times I *must* be successful!" "I *must* be young forever!" "The world *must* work the way I want!" These dogmas often lead to serious trouble!

Frances wanted — and demanded — more freedom from Frank's control than she actually had. On the other hand, Frank wanted — and demanded — an obedient wife, which he felt he didn't have. Both wanted — and demanded — more "respect" from the other than either was actually getting.

Frances wanted freedom to choose to stay in or to leave the marriage, but was afraid to give herself this choice. With her views she could not happily stay *or* leave. If she left, she thought she couldn't survive. If she stayed, she thought she would make herself miserable forever. She perceived herself to be stuck, as if she had no choice. She was very aware of her "stuckness," but she did not clearly see that she was creating it by making herself terrified about living alone.

Frank also demanded, both consciously and unconsciously, a guarantee he did not, of course, have — that Frances would never leave him. He also "needed" — and again, did not have — a guarantee of emotional support. He demanded that he *should not, must not,* be required to change himself or end their marriage, and he insisted that Frances *must not* leave either.

Let's challenge this couple's irrational *shoulds* and *musts*. *Must* life conform to what Frank and Frances each demand? *Must* "reality" be the way they insist it be? No. We can find no reason whatever! The laws of nature seem to operate impersonally, regardless of what any of us *want*, and regardless of what this wife and husband *demand*. "Time and chance happeneth to them all" *(Ecclesiastes 9:11)*.

Gravity gives no regard for our wants. We do better by accepting its laws than by raging against them. We have learned to work with gravity when walking on earth, flying airplanes, and traveling in outer-space, and — as Isaac Newton discovered from the lump on his head — when sitting under fruit trees in late summer. Until the twentieth century, gravity seemed certain to prevent us from flying, but with experimentation and testing, we have made incredible progress!

Similarly, with experimentation and testing, we can learn to work with "human nature" to solve previously "unsolvable" communication problems. We can improve our relationships by working *with* human behavior — giving up our demands and sticking to our preferences. We can then experimentally change our experiences and converse better with each other.

Frank, as shown in his letter in chapter 2, found it difficult to distinguish between "reality" and his demands for things to conform to his wishes. Many people have this difficulty. When he finally saw the distinction, he also applied it to other important situations. As a professor, his students once feared him. Now that he has used REBT to give up his demands that they absolutely must act a certain way, he enjoys his students, inviting them into his office to visit. Instead of avoiding him, they now seek him out; he's become a popular teacher!

Another example is Frank's work area. When he went into his basement and saw all his unfinished projects, he used to feel depressed. He was overwhelmed by having too much to do, and the horror of never getting it all done. Now, when he goes into his basement, he thinks, "How lucky I am. I'll always have something interesting to do."

What made that difference? In Frank's words, "Guideline 1 is broader than just accepting the other 'as is.' It really applies to accepting people, things, and *situations* 'as is.' When I accepted the problem of all those unfinished projects, I realized that if I had completed them all, I might have felt bored with life. I would have nothing to look forward to doing. Now, I always have something pleasurable to look forward to doing."

Frank expanded his growing applications of Guideline 1 to his disagreements with others. He used to feel angry with differences and disagreements because they were so "stupid" when he was so "obviously" right. Now, they provide him with the pleasure of learning and growing, a challenge to explore and resolve. "I like challenges," he asserts.

Good Communication Starts With Acceptance
To communicate better, we can acknowledge — and accept — the "nature" of the universe; it seems to include no "absolute" *shoulds, musts,* or *oughts.* In "nature" there is no difference between the way

something "is" and the way it *should, must,* or *ought* to be. If it *should* be a certain way, it *automatically* is the way it *should* be. The universe does not follow human desires, nor make personal evaluations of itself. But we humans often do evaluate or measure What Is Going On, (WIGO), in the world, and we frequently fail to notice the discrepancy between the *reality* of the way things are, and the way we say they absolutely *should, must,* or *ought* to be. We *prefer* things to be *better,* and we also often *demand* that social and external events follow our preferences.

REBT has a special label for words and phrases that express or imply "absolutistic" demands: *"musturbation."* We humans usually do not use musturbatory words (absolutistic shoulds and musts) when things are going the way we like them to go. We mostly use absolutistic musts when we observe a significant difference between (1) What Is Going On, (WIGO), and (2) what we want.

WIGO is another way to talk about "reality." "Reality" is another word for "truth." When we talk about "reality," whose view of "reality" or "truth" are we using? Your view or my view? When our views differ, is your view of "reality" subjective and therefore "false," and my view of "reality" objective and therefore "true?" Our differences create both a philosophical and a practical problem. Included in the core of almost all of our arguments, fights, conflicts, or power struggles, there seems to be a difference or disagreement about "what is reality."

"You're selfish!"
"No, I'm not."
"Yes, you are!"
"No, I'm not!"
"You are, too!"
"No, it's not I who is selfish. It's you who are selfish!"

Who is right? Who holds the truth? What is the "reality" in this dispute? What is going on here?

Rational Emotive Behavior Therapy (REBT) holds that each of us experiences "reality" or "truth" according to the viewpoint of our own belief system, i.e., our own *concept* of "reality" and "truth." Your "reality" or "truth" is not identical to my mental model of "reality" or "truth." Our viewpoints may be somewhat similar, but our ways of construing or understanding "reality" or "truth" are hardly identical. The differences we create are likely and "normal."

Shoulds and Musts As Crazy-Makers

In a "real" sense, our absolutistic shoulds and musts are "crazy-makers." Why? Because they both acknowledge and deny the same "reality" at the same time. Blaming is an example. Frances complained that Frank shouldn't put her down. She complained and blamed; in her mind, the "fact" was that he did put her down. Her complaint, "He should not disrespect me!" acknowledges the "fact" that he did put her down. But her emotional "reality" — what she felt — was that he must not do what he, in fact, did. Frances insisted that she couldn't take it any more, but she continued to take it, contrary to her assertion. Perhaps what she meant is that she won't take it any more, and was getting ready to leave the marriage. Her "reality" was her upsetness. When she felt upset, Frances's must ("He must not upset me!") denied her "reality" — that Frank was upsetting her!

This paradox, taking what should not exist but does exist, is confusing because we usually do not acknowledge it. Frequently we present our should to ourselves as if it were absolute reality. We are convinced it is obvious that What Is Going On, (WIGO), should not exist, and What Should Go On, (WSGO), should exist. We do not examine the conflict between WIGO, what is going on, and WSGO, what should go on. WSGO is "obviously" not WIGO. Therefore, the should that we see as "self-evident" is largely fictional and, in a "real" sense, doesn't exist at all! Our preferences (and Frances's preferences) exist as preferences, but our absolutistic shoulds (like Frances's) are contradicted by "reality."

Therefore at one and the same time, her should denies the reality it claims and acknowledges. This crazy-making happens with Frank's shoulds, too!

Did Mr. and Mrs. Jones uniquely accept each other when they had a real, unresolved disagreement? We are convinced that they really did. They achieved one of the main goals of this book — to show you how to fully (and non-blamingly!) accept others' disagreements, and how to actually enjoy most differences that you have with others.

"I'm Not Wrong, You Are!"

As we help scores of clients (not to mention friends and relatives) learn to use REBT to alleviate their difficulties, we find that the first demand of people is that their perception or concept of "reality" *must* not be wrong or inconsistent. Thus, they may decide that it is "right" to be honest with others and will not allow themselves to use the slightest "white lie." They will tell a child that they are going away on a short trip to prevent her from being very distraught about the truth that they will be away on a long trip. Later they will mercilessly beat themselves because they absolutely *should have* told the child the complete truth. They insist they always, at all times, have to be "right" and "proper," even though at times they aren't.

A common dilemma for marital partners is to think, "Because my partner is married to me, and because he presumably loves me and understands me, he *absolutely should* see that I am right and should go along with me!" Faint hope! Your mate may truly love you and honor you, but being of a different sex, reared dissimilarly, and unique in several innate ways, will therefore easily see things his or her way.

Zack, one of Al's clients, was a real feminist, believing that men were no better than women, and that women should be given equal rights.

But he still believed that his wife, Dora, was obliged to agree with him on important matters. He loved her, and felt she should in return "prove" her love for him by this kind of agreement. I showed him that he was really discriminating against her with this view because, if they were truly equal, he would always have to agree with her on important matters, which obviously, he didn't.

Zack saw that his marital relationship with Dora made it highly *preferable* for them to agree on important matters — but not *obligatory*. No matter how "right" he was about any issue, Dora didn't have to see his "rightness." When they both accepted their disagreements, even when they thought the other "wrong," they soon found that they had a more agreeable relationship. [AE]

Communication

What is communication? Simply stated, it is the sending and receiving of information or messages. Specifically, when you communicate, you first try to influence other people through talking and other forms of discourse. Second, you try to induce them to listen to you, respond to you, agree with you, and pretty much do what you would like them to do.

What is your purpose when you communicate? Let's be honest: mainly to influence others to give you more of what you want, and less of what you don't want. But let's also be practical and clearly distinguish between *influencing* others to see things your way, and *demanding* that they *absolutely must* do what you desire. You may have many wants: attention, approval, love, sex, money, friendship, companionship, enjoyable intimacy, and more. You can even want better communication!

Rational Emotive Behavior Therapy helps you communicate by showing you how to stay with your wants and preferences, and refusing to raise them to demands and compulsions. When you demand, you resort to "MUSTurbation" by: (1) insisting that people or things *must* be the way you *want* them to be; and, (2) by feeling upset when your commands are not fulfilled as they absolutely should be! You may express your demands openly or directly: "You *must* give me this! You *must not* deprive me of that!" Or you may express them more subtly and indirectly, such as showing people that you feel hurt, angry, or depressed when they ignore your *musts* and *commands*.

You free yourself emotionally and communicate better when you honestly admit that you are trying to *compel* others to see and do things your way. You free yourself even more when you *surrender* your demands, and stop trying to compel others to do what you want them to do. Then you *really* communicate.

Frances and Frank do not have perfect communication, but now they enjoy their differences, which they often work through easily and quickly. Not always, but much more frequently than they did before Frank discovered how to fully accept people, things, and situations "as is."

Practical Problems and Emotional Problems

Like Frank and Frances, Thelma and Sol, Zack and Dora, and most people, you tend to have two basic kinds of problems: practical problems and emotional problems. Your practical problem is how to get what you want. Your emotional problem is how to refuse to upset yourself when you don't get what you want. You will find this distinction between your practical problems and emotional problems highly useful when you apply REBT to your life.

Your emotional problem — the *demand* that you must have good communication — will sabotage solving your practical problem — *how* to communicate well with others. What's more, such a demand tends to block you from solving other practical problems as well. Your "musturbation" adds another problem to the practical problem you already have — giving you two problems for the price of one!

If you make yourself feel *disturbed* because you don't get the kind of communication you want, you create an emotional problem about communicating. And what creates this disturbance? Your compulsive demand that you *must* have "acceptable" communication!

When you are able to give up such absolutistic demands and accept the reality and limitations of yourself, your partner, and your life circumstances, you've created a solid foundation for the good communication you desire. Musturbation about communication will very likely result in continued poor communication!

We think you'll find your communication and your relationships will get a lot better if you learn to use our *Seven Guidelines for Great Relationships.* You'll meet all seven in the next chapter.

4

Seven Guidelines
for Great Relationships

and Better Communication

Michelle was so impressed, when Ted told her about Frank's use of the Seven Guidelines with his wife, that she decided to learn to use them in her love relationship with Hunter.

Here is one example of her difficulties with him that she wanted to handle better. Michelle and Hunter were on their way to a little league baseball game to cheer for her son. Hunter wanted Michelle to agree that she would not separate from him or get sidetracked into conversations with her friends at the game. She agreed. He implied that he would do the same for her. If both had kept their agreement as the other understood it, we wouldn't have this soap opera to share with you.

Their tempest in a teapot also could also have been avoided if even one of them had used the principles of Rational Emotive Behavior Therapy. If *both* had used the REBT sharing methods, their disagreement could probably have been confronted and handled immediately. But then, of course, we would not have the following fine example of their difficulties.

On the way into the ballpark, Hunter saw a food stand and left Michelle to go buy a hot dog. In the meantime, she found a place to sit on the grass and, while waiting for him, was joined by a woman friend. The friend had a stiff neck and Michelle offered to massage her friend's neck while waiting for Hunter to return.

Michelle continued to massage her friend's neck for some time after Hunter had joined them on the grass. He became angry and upset over Michelle's "broken promise." He felt betrayed, and he gave her an ultimatum: if she didn't "get her act together" by the end of the month, he would leave her. For Hunter there was no

The Seven Guidelines for Great Relationships and Better Communication

1. *Accept your partner "as is."* Avoid blaming. Determine that you are in your relationship to enjoy yourself, not to try to fix, reform, or straighten out your partner. Be responsible for your own feelings. Allow yourself to influence your partner, but do not demand that he or she must change. Also, give her or him the freedom to influence you. Yes, to persuade and inform you.

2. *Express appreciation frequently.* Avoid steady criticism. Acknowledge your partner often for small things. Find, discover, or even create things you really value about your partner. Say them. Honesty is important here. Avoid the main relationship "killer" — frequent criticism of your partner.

3. *Communicate from integrity.* Be honest regarding beliefs and evidence that conflict with your own views of what is happening. When your partner is right, admit it. Be both honest and tactful. Allow different perceptions to exist. Agree to stop penalizing each other for your honesty as you now often may do. Agree that both of you will be honest and let the other "get away" with honesty.

4. *Share and explore differences with your partner.*

difference for them to share. As far as he was concerned, Michelle "didn't have a side" in the disagreement. The gap between her "agreement" and her "betrayal," as far as Hunter was concerned, was huge, and he would fight over it and possibly use it to justify leaving the relationship.

Hunter's perception of Michelle's motives illustrates his tunnel vision at that moment. In his mind, he was *totally* right and Michelle was *totally* wrong. He was the "victim" of Michelle's broken agreement. There was only one way to view the situation — his way. He did *not* explore what her side might be because, "obviously," she didn't have a valid side to explore. Michelle saw that she had no "right" to have her own side if it differed from Hunter's. They got through this upset with a great deal of unresolved emotional pain.

Three Relationship Roles

There are three possible roles in a relationship: one-up, one-down, or a peer partnership. The goal in using our *Guidelines* is to move from a "one-up and one-down" toward a "peer" or "equal" partnership. Let us point out here that Frank was dominant — or one-up — in his relationship with Frances, while Michelle took a one-down position with Hunter, unintentionally supporting his one-up position with her. Michelle's one-down position, however, was eventually reworked by using the *Seven Guidelines*. As she began to accept Hunter "as is," she was able to reframe her perception of her own one-downness to a position closer to "equality" with Hunter. She also recognized that she had some choices about how she might respond to his behavior. Recognizing that she had choices allowed her to feel *less* one-down; she no longer felt that she must conform to his wishes.

Do you see how you might use these Guidelines if you were in Michelle's position? Michelle didn't and phoned Ted for help.

The ideas behind the Seven Guidelines have been around a long time. These Seven Guidelines, mostly (but not exclusively) based on REBT, were organized into a system in 1986 by Ted and Jolanta to serve as the foundation for their marriage. Building on the version that Frank used, in this chapter we present the full version of the *Seven Guidelines* that Michelle decided to learn how to use.

Explore disagreements with your partner to move toward a higher resolution that accepts parts of both your views. Or, to agree to disagree. Additionally, be ready to compromise without pretending that you agree when you really don't agree.

5. *Support your partner's goals.* Don't surrender your own integrity and your own important desires and views, but go as far as you honestly can to support your partner even when you clearly disagree.

6. *Give your partner the right to be wrong.* Respect *both* of your rights to be fallible humans — your inalienable right to make mistakes and to learn from your own experiences and errors. Don't honor only *your* own right to be an error-prone human!

7. *Reconsider your wants as goals* that you may achieve later. (This is a guideline that enables you to work properly with the other six guidelines.) When you don't get what you want or desire, remind yourself that you *don't have* to get what you want, now or ever!

NOTE: Choose to practice the *Seven Guidelines* as a unilateral commitment regardless of what your partner does or doesn't do. Each time you have not succeeded, look to discover a mistake you may have made. You also may have something significant to learn about your way of talking or listening.

Michelle's Letter to Ted

Here is what Michelle wrote to Ted about her experiences with the Guidelines:

As I write about my personal experience with the Seven Guidelines, I think that I could categorize my life as "BG" and "AG" — Before the Guidelines and After the Guidelines. Hunter and I married after I started using the Seven Guidelines.

Before my exposure to REBT, on which the Guidelines were based, my life could be characterized as basic "victimhood" — everything "was" as a result of "things that happened." I was simply the victim of all the things that happened to me. I didn't see that I had *choice* or any particular say in the matter.

I left my first marriage because of the things my husband was *doing* and *not doing* that I felt caused me great pain and unhappiness. I thought that finding Hunter, my second husband, was the answer to my problems because he seemed to understand me so well and was willing to truly listen to me and "get with me." Imagine my surprise when I began to have some of the same problems with Hunter as I had had with Jerry! Could the "problem" be in me? My coming to that realization was what allowed me to engage in my conversations with you, Ted, and commit myself to working with the Seven Guidelines.

I'm unclear whether it was the guidelines or the actual talking with you that was most helpful to me. Most likely, it was the combination of the two. In any case, my exposure to you, Hunter, and the Seven Guidelines was like learning a new language. I had glimpses of this "language" at other times in my life, through what I call the "spiritual writings" by people such as Jesus, Buddha, and Ram Dass, but they had only been fleeting glimpses that would give me a very nice feeling as I read the words, and would disappear whenever a tough situation arose in my life. As I began to work with you and Hunter, and ultimately with the Seven Guidelines, I started seeing my own contribution to problems in my life, and thus discovered a process that I could sink my teeth into and get more of the results I wanted.

It was with great interest — and not a little dismay at first — that I noticed that when I would call you in the midst of a huge upset with Hunter, that you would not agree with me — as I wanted you to do — about how bad Hunter was. Instead, you would understand my sense of despair, but without blaming Hunter, almost as if Hunter was only a minor player in the script. The focus would almost always be on me, what I was thinking or saying to myself that made me upset and miserable.

I find Guideline 1, accepting your partner "as is," to be the most useful guideline when I make myself disturbed. Accepting Hunter "as is" has allowed me to stay in the relationship long enough to see how I contribute to what doesn't work for us. I now see "his problems" as "our problems," and our upsets have consequently become much less frequent and less disruptive. I don't need to change him; instead I look at why we aren't experiencing the happiness and joy that I know is possible in our relationship.

Guideline 4, sharing differences with the intention of a win-win, has been a difficult one for me, as well as for Hunter. Right now we see the demands we resort to when we disagree; and seeing them is actually helpful. But we haven't yet successfully found a way to share our differences and willingly move into that win-win third position that fits for both of us and allows us to avoid upset and drama.

Recently, in our latest upset, I thought that I had had a breakthrough in my thinking about Guideline 4 (sharing differences with the intention of a win-win), and I began to write about it. However, when I got near the end of telling my story, I suddenly realized that Hunter's position had some validity. I had been sticking staunchly to my position with a lot of support from the outside world, and that was what had kept me from empathically understanding Hunter's position his way and ultimately allowing us to work through our differences. The wind went out of my sails, so to speak, as I sat writing my story, and I wasn't able to finish it. I saw my need to be right. Eventually, we were able to work through this upset.

To me, the Seven Guidelines are a work of brilliance in looking at relationships. Each guideline is a specific step or approach that can be actively applied in most relationships. But Guideline 7, make your want into a future goal, is the "cream of the crop" in my estimation. It is the one that makes all the others do-able, because it allows for all the human mistakes that I am bound to make — and have consistently made — in my life. It is still a huge challenge for me to make a goal out of those situations that are not what I would like them to be. However, using this approach seems to make life more fun and less nerve-shattering — something that I would like to experience more easily. I still see barriers as a negative factor, rather than as encouragement toward a goal. I will feel as if I have "graduated" when I can experience a barrier in my life as a challenge to a new goal. I want to use Guideline 7 cheerfully, as well as use the other six guidelines.

Reading the draft of this book has given me such a sense of comfort during this time of great upheaval in my life. It is my sense of having a *choice* that comes to me so strongly through your words. I find that very comforting. [Michelle]

~ ~ ~

As of this writing, Michelle is doing considerably better in accepting her right to be herself and not put herself down. However, she is still having difficulty in the successful sharing of disagreements with Hunter. Later we will look further at the difficulties many people seem to have with sharing disagreements.

Do you remember the old story about the princess and the frog? When the princess kissed the frog, she broke the "magic" spell that imprisoned him in the form of a frog. Upon being freed, he sprang into view as her handsome Prince Charming.

Most of us seem "trapped" in some role that is not "really" us. Metaphorically speaking, we are frogs — or Sleeping Beauties — waiting for that magic someone to free us.

Our Seven Guidelines are not as easy to use as a kiss, but they do work — *if you work them!* They help you become a more integrated human, and can change both your view of your partner and of yourself; *almost* making you into a prince or princess. Until you try the Seven Guidelines, you may have trouble believing that they can really work.

Let's go back to Frank, who was angry with Frances because "she wastes too much time talking on the telephone." Later he wrote:

Concerning the concept of the frog and the princess, my life with Frances has changed drastically for the better, but it took some time. I would attribute this to talking with you, Ted, about the Seven

Guidelines, and applying them to myself. I was, of course, unable to apply them perfectly, but I kept trying. At first, I got small results in my relationship with Frances. Then I began to change in other ways, too. Thinking about Frances differently made a big change in how I felt about myself and the world around me. Frances began to respond more positively, and that helped me spiral upwards! Sometimes I wish I could explain this REBT method to others. Often they do not have the time to talk, but if they listened, it might help them! [Frank]

When he wrote his letter, Frank had worked his way up to Guideline 4. Remember that Frances was miserable in their marriage. Most of her friends urged her to divorce Frank because, in their view, Frank would *never* change. Frances agreed that he would never change and that she would leave when she was "ready." Since Frank's work with the Seven Guidelines, although she still sees remaining problems in their marriage, she no longer considers divorce. Even though Frank has not yet completed his exploration of Guidelines 5, 6, and 7, she has now fallen in love with him all over again!

While she and Hunter were engaged, Michelle heard about how Frank had improved his marriage. She committed herself to try the Seven Guidelines, even though Hunter did not choose to do so with her. As it turned out, both Frank's wife Frances and Hunter decided later to try the guidelines — at least *some* of the time.

Let's look more closely at what Frank did to change his marriage with Frances so profoundly.

First, Frank learned about — and envied — what Ted already had: a supportive wife. Ted told him that her support greatly increased after they used the guidelines together. Frank decided to learn how to work with them. Second, Frank set up definite procedures for learning one guideline at a time, starting with number 1. Third, he talked with Ted over the phone once every two weeks about his progress.

Frank immediately ran into difficulty when he tried to adopt Guideline 1. He made himself angry at Frances, and did not accept her "as is" when she did something he really didn't like. Then he put himself down as a failure and a "no-goodnik" for not accepting her "as is," and thereby made himself feel depressed and hopeless. He obviously didn't accept *himself* "as is." However, in spite of his "failures," Frances reported that Frank's anger had decreased.

By trying to follow Guideline 1, Frank learned that his *shoulds* and *musts* were *demands*, and that his *demands* also included *shoulds* and *musts*. He was demanding that Frances should and must conform to his wishes. In that way, he made her an extension of him, instead of letting her be herself. Thinking about this, he discovered that he loved her for being herself! He then decided that he didn't really want her to conform to his demands. He wanted her to choose to change some of her behavior for her own growth, and not as a response to his demands. He began actually to admire her willingness to stand up to him and to defy his demands.

After a time, Frank realized that his demandingness — his *shoulds* and *musts* — conflicted with reality. Frances was Frances. She was herself, and not what he demanded she be. When he realized this and saw her in the light of Guideline 1 (non-blamingly accept your partner "as-is"), he realized that a good communication engineer accepts social — as well as physical — reality to help solve problems in his marriage. So Frank's first job for improving his marriage was non-blamingly to accept Frances "as is." He also realized that Guideline 1 is basic to all the other communication and relationship guidelines. By accepting Frances "as is," and himself "as is," Frank found all the rest of the guidelines much easier to apply.

Michelle had a similar experience using Guideline 1 with Hunter. She thought she understood this guideline and had mastered it enough to go on to the other guidelines. But she learned that she had to return to Guideline 1 again and again in order to absorb it. Michelle found it especially difficult when Hunter failed to accept her "as is." She absolutely felt he "always" *should* and *must* accept her "as is."

Why did Michelle keep working again and again on accepting Hunter "as is"? Because she felt much better within herself, and she liked the results of having done so. She became optimistic about changing their relationship, and found that Hunter changed when she changed. Previously she had put herself into the double bind of having to control Hunter and herself. Now she only worked at controlling herself. As yet, Hunter has not decided to use the Seven Guidelines consistently. However, he volunteered to memorize them, and appreciated Michelle reading them to him.

Note that in the two couples we are discussing, only one person from each partnership committed to follow the guidelines, but the other partner — and the relationship — also improved.

You may benefit from even partial use of the Guidelines. Of course, you're likely to communicate even better when you and your partner mutually apply all of them. Guideline 1 seems to be the most important — learning and practicing non-blaming acceptance of your partner and yourself "as is" — and is the foundation for the other six guidelines.

Clarice's Difficulties with Harry

Clarice was a 35-year-old teacher who used REBT quite well in dealing with her anxiety about her work and graduate school courses. Before REBT, she had to perform almost perfectly in both areas and was enormously self-demeaning if she even slightly failed to do so. After using REBT for awhile, she was able to unconditionally accept herself when she got a "C" in an important course, and when her principal criticized her about her unruly classroom. In both instances she felt disappointed with her behavior, but not with herself. These were important victories for her and showed that she really was getting some of the central principles of REBT.

Clarice then wanted to work on her relationship with Harry, her difficult fiancé, whom she was hesitant to marry. Harry — though he had worked as an accountant for ten years — had not saved a penny. He gambled frequently, and sometimes borrowed money from Clarice.

Clarice used REBT to stop being angry and depressed about her relationship with Harry, and it improved considerably. Their engagement was still rocky, however, so when she heard that Al and Ted were writing a book on communication guidelines, she asked Al to go over the Seven Guidelines with her. She worked at the Guidelines for several weeks and became less angry and depressed about Harry's behavior, although she was still determined to break their engagement if he did not reduce his criticism and quit gambling. She would give him three months to work on these problems, or else!

This was a notable change in Clarice, because previously she had a "dire need" for Harry's love, but now replaced this need with a strong preference — and a strong determination to break up with him if he didn't significantly change. Great!

As Al points out, however, the story didn't end there…

I asked Clarice what about how using the Seven Guidelines for better communication contributed to her decreased anger and depression, and her determined confronting of Harry. She said the guidelines gave her more specific ways of adding to her REBT, and they fleshed out some of the main REBT principles.

"In what ways did they do so?" I asked.

"Well, I first used Guideline 1 and I fully accepted Harry 'as is'" Clarice replied. "This is the same as the REBT principle, 'Accept others unconditionally.' I realized more than ever the value of this idea, and I specifically worked on accepting Harry, but not his criticism — especially of others, like my parents — and not at all his gambling."

"So you accepted the sinner, but not the sin," I suggested.

"Yes. Then I used Guideline 2 to give Harry frequent appreciation. I appreciated his good points, such as his ambition and hard work. This I thought followed the REBT line of not overgeneralizing and labeling. He was too critical and gambled recklessly, but he was not *only* that kind of behavior. He also had good points, which I not only saw, but went out of my way to point out. I forced myself, which I had rarely done before, to tell him unangrily that I thought gambling was stupid and destructive. But I again made it clear that he was not a stupid person. Using REBT, I refused to overgeneralize again."

"And how about Guideline 4, 'share your differences and try to gain a win-win outcome'?" I asked.

"I'm not sure about that, but I think I did my best. I didn't want to hurt Harry, but I thought that if I were firm and insisted that he stop gambling, that would not only be good for me, but would also be very good for him. So in that sense we would have a win-win position. At least I didn't condemn him for his gambling. So I did my best."

"Guideline 5, 'support your partner's aims and purposes, and goals,' were you able to put that to work?" I asked.

"No," Clarice said. "I would have lost my 'integrity' (or self-respect) if I supported Harry's gambling goals. So I insisted that he stop gambling. But I didn't put him down for it. I again used REBT's unconditional other-acceptance, and accepted *him*, but I was not going to accept his gambling. And, again, I didn't get angry at him, just firm about his gambling."

"Did you use Guideline 6, 'give your partner the right to be wrong'?"

"Yes, I used it in principle to let Harry be what he was, if he still insisted on gambling, but not with me as his wife. I would still be his friend, and never, never condemn him. This, it seems to me, is still REBT's unconditional other-acceptance, even if I lost him and failed to induce him to give up gambling."

Clarice was sticking to REBT's "UOA" and "USA" (see chapter 2), but still maintaining her integrity, and basically following the guidelines, too.

"How about Guideline 7, 'if you don't get what you want, consider your want as a goal to be achieved later'?"

"My goals are to get Harry to be less critical and to stop gambling. If I don't achieve them now, I'll try to achieve them later. If I never achieve them with Harry, I'll keep trying with another more suitable partner. This, I think, follows the REBT principle of having high frustration tolerance, of not awfulizing about what I can't have right now, and of working determinedly to get it later."

"Right!" I concluded. "You seem to be using the Seven Guidelines and at the same time following some of the main REBT principles. Good luck!"

Actually, Clarice had bad luck. Harry kept falling back to heavy gambling and she broke off their engagement. But she did so without rage and depression. [AE]

Interpersonal relationships are rarely simple, however! Ted offers this different perspective on Clarice's situation:

Clarice rightly wasn't clear about Guideline 4. Her "win-win" was an *if* Harry does what she wants, *then* it would be a win-win. An "if-then" is not the same as a "win-win." An *if* then could be a win for Clarice, but it could be conformity for Harry. A win-win happens when each one experiences a win. In Al's dialogue with her, there is no mention of exploring Harry's side of her issue. In effect, what she did was to assert her side as an ultimatum for Harry to stop gambling, or else she would not marry him. There was no hint of a mutual sharing of their disagreement or differences around her issue, or his issue for that matter. So, in effect, she did not thoroughly and effectively use Guideline 4, in spite of her good intentions.

We purposely phrased Guideline 4 to include "share and explore," because most people, like Clarice, seem to equate *assertion* with sharing, and leave out *exploring* entirely. It is useful for people to include sharing as assertion, and also explore the other's side. "Because I don't agree with you, would you do me the favor of telling me more of your side?"

If you genuinely wish to communicate with other people, you want to know why they believe or think the way they do. What experiences lead to their conclusion? What conflicting beliefs or opinions do they have? What are their conflicts around the beliefs they have?

There is a whole new world of discovery if you choose to explore your partner's side of your issue. How did Harry get into gambling in the first place? What does gambling mean to Harry? What is Harry's story? Did Clarice explore these kinds of questions with Harry? Apparently not. When we get into another's story as an exploration, we almost always can find something in common that presents the possibility of moving toward a win-win. It is even easier and more fun when the exploring is a mutual-exchange activity.

Clarice made her choice, but her story might have had a different ending if she had used Guideline 4 more effectively. [TC]

We're now going to look at each of the Seven Guidelines in detail, beginning with the next chapter.

5

Guideline 1:
Accept Your Partner "As Is"

Accept your partner "as is." Avoid blaming. Determine that you are in your relationship to enjoy yourself, not to try to fix, reform, or straighten out your partner. Be responsible for your own feelings. Allow yourself to influence your partner, but do not demand that he or she must change. Also, give her or him the freedom to influence you. Yes, to persuade and inform you.

In this guideline we wish to influence you to change your paradigm: your way of thinking, evaluating, interpreting, and communicating.

And what is a *paradigm?* Borrowing from Joan Jordan Porter, a colleague of Ted's, your paradigm is the lens you look through to see the world around you. It includes your core values, priorities, ethics and rules, as well as the methods for using them. If you did not have a way to organize the millions of bits of information that come your way every moment of your life, you would be unable to function in the world. You cannot function without a way of thinking, a paradigm.

Your paradigm pre-sorts, and makes selections, *before* you consciously notice elements in your world. Although there is some variation about how you sort out and select the elements, these variations occur within the boundaries of how you think social reality works.

You can change your paradigm, i.e., *the way you are organizing the multitude of data around you.* When you change your opinions, and your wording, to be more accurate with your experiences, you are likely changing your paradigm in small ways that may accumulate into big changes in your understanding of WIGO (What Is Going On).

Note that in addition to each of us having our individual paradigms, our families, communities, groups, and societies also have paradigms. Our society's predominant paradigm — or general attitude — sets the tone for what is accepted and acceptable, and what is considered "common sense."

For the most part, what makes up a paradigm can be uncovered if we look for what we assume is "the way it is."

Although there is some latitude in setting society's standards for "the way it is," there are also limits. For example, for centuries, society's paradigm included the belief that the earth was the center of the universe and that the sun and planets orbited around it. No matter how fiercely the people believed, the astronomers calculated, and the authorities demanded compliance, the universe did not change its configuration to agree with society's paradigm. However, no paradigm is a perfect match with "out there." Some are less perfect than others.

We especially suggest changing your stated and unstated *shoulds* and *musts* to fully acknowledging reality "as is," and changing your victim ways of thinking and feeling, from your assumptions of "You hurt me," or "You made me angry," to thinking, "I chose to hurt me," or "I chose to make myself angry about the 'wrong' things you did."

> Whenever I feel angry at the therapists we supervise at the Albert Ellis Institute in New York, when I think they have acted "stupidly" with their clients, I remind myself, "Yes, *they* may have behaved stupidly, but *I* chose to anger myself against them. First, let me replace my anger at *them* with displeasure at their *acts,* then let me see if I can unangrily correct them." Sometimes, not always, I do this in time to diplomatically correct them. If not, I review my anger in my mind, correct it later, and prepare for the next therapist "stupidity." [AE]

You Have the Right to Influence Others

You definitely have the right to influence your partner. Why? Because, really, you cannot *not* influence others.

Think about this for a moment: even inanimate objects can influence human behavior. Consider a table in the middle of a room. You want to walk across the room to pick up a book. When you walk, you do not walk straight across the room. Instead you walk around the table because you don't know how to walk through it. The table didn't consciously *do* anything to influence you. It innocently stayed in the middle of the room. It did not *cause* you to walk around it, either. You *chose* to walk around it in order to get what you wanted. Nor did the table *cause* you to want the book. Yet, the mere existence of the table in the same room with you influenced your behavior.

Similarly, you influence your partner's behavior, whether or not you realize it. Everything you do, and do not do, just by your very presence, exerts an influence. You may often be too busy blaming others to perceive your own influence on them. You may only see that they "wrongly" affect *you!*

If an inanimate object such as a table can influence you, how much greater can a live human being (or a dead human, for that matter) sway you? A partner who is doing more than merely existing, but also acting, talking, and trying to impress you, will influence you even more, will he not? And the same goes for your influencing him.

Since you do affect others, no matter what you do, you might as well seek to influence your partner to act the ways you prefer. Michelle was sometimes so focused on not demanding or controlling Hunter that she entirely neglected this part of Guideline 1, "Allow yourself to influence your partner." If you use this guideline, you respect and non-blamingly accept your partner "as is," and you accept his right, as a separate person, to want what he wants. But you *also* try to influence your partner to go in the direction that you favor.

Avoid trying to *control* your partner by demanding or commanding that he or she *should* or *must* conform to your wishes and wants. When you accept *what is going on* with your partner "as is," you refrain from upsetting yourself when he does not behave or feel the way you want. When you are feeling seriously upset about your relationship, perhaps you are sneaking in a demand that you must change, fix, reform, or straighten out your partner. Check that demand!

Give Your Partner the Freedom to Influence You

What is sauce for the goose is also sauce for the gander. Turnabout, says another old saw, is fair play. Unfortunately, you may often try to influence your mate, and resist or resent her seeking to influence you. You may take pride in being "yourself." "I am me, and nobody has the right to change me, or even to try to change me." "The way I am now is me, forever. If I change the way I am, I am no longer me."

Note here your irrational refusal to acknowledge the fact that you are constantly changing from birth to death, no matter what you do. Change is not just a matter of choice, but automatic, a given constant. You can often choose, though not absolutely choose, how you change. But change itself is an inevitable fact of life.

Unfortunately, you can view *influence* and *control* as if they were the same thing, which they are not. You cannot *not* be influenced. However, you can choose whether to accept or not accept your partner's particular influence. When you distinguish between influence and control, you usually add to your ability to achieve "self-control." You give yourself the right to influence others, and give them the right to influence you.

To recover your equilibrium after you respond with an emotional disturbance to another's demand, try to reframe the demand as a suggestion or "influence." Don't keep disturbing yourself by framing a mere suggestion as a command that you *should* or *must* "obey." However, you may respond inconsistently from one situation to another, as the following example will show.

Michelle *sometimes* responds to Hunter's demands, or even his suggestions, as *commands* that she *must* obey. She then acts indecisively, or weakly accedes to his commands. She feels bad about herself for being so weak and insecure, and has an inner conflict between obeying Hunter and "being herself." At other times, Michelle frames Hunter's suggestions as suggestions, and even reframes his demands or commands as mere *suggestions* to consider. Then she is much more in control of herself, and as a result seeks less to control him.

You can react to your partner's efforts to control you in four main ways:
- *Go with* the suggestion or demand.
- *Go against* the suggestion or demand.
- *Ignore* the suggestion.

- *Try to explore* and *negotiate* the terms of the suggestion or demand. (You can even go along with a part of what your partner wants from you, while going against another part.)

Whether you choose to go with or against your partner's wants, you'd better consider your options and select one that you honestly think is right, valid, or useful. That is, right, valid, or useful for *you*. But be wary of selecting an option based on one or more of your *shoulds.*

If you think you *absolutely should* or *must* go with your partner's desires, you unassertively conform and surrender your autonomy. Your underlying attitude here is usually something like, "I *have to* conform to what my partner wants in order to survive happily — or to survive at all." "I *must not* rock the boat." "I *must* smooth things over." You are choosing "cowardly" conformity.

On the other hand, if you rebelliously refuse to do what your mate wants, you may believe, "I *must* be myself" — sometimes with the added condition "even if it kills me."

You can avoid both over-conformity and over-rebellion and decide to go with another's want because you honestly *agree* that following her suggestion is a good idea. You then are "yourself," without being a victim of your own rigid *shoulds* or *musts*. If you honestly *disagree* with another's suggestions or demands and you choose — without *shoulds* or *musts* — to go against his wants, you are also yourself. When you choose this flexible way, you act firmly and autonomously.

In real life, at one time or another, we all tend to use each of the three basic responses described above: over-conforming, over-rebellious, and flexibly autonomous. Our Seven Guidelines for communication aim to help you *reduce* both your over-conformity and over-rebellion, in favor of *increasing* your flexible autonomy.

To repeat: *over-conforming* follows, "I *must* do what my partner wants me to do." *Over-rebellion* follows, "I *must* go against what he or she wants me to do." *Flexible autonomy* follows, "I choose, without *shoulds* or *musts,* to go with, or go against, what my partner wants me to do, by following my own best judgment." Instead of acting in the extreme by conforming *to* or rebelling *against* your partner, you autonomously (but flexibly) give him or her the right to influence you, without controlling you.

Even better than *passively* giving your partner the right to influence you, you can *actively* support his right to do so.

Al has seen hundreds of couples for marriage and family counseling since 1943 — well over a half century! Almost all of them had marriages that were in serious trouble because one or both partners were ignoring Guideline 1: *Accept your partner "as is." Avoid blaming.*

Sometimes, of course, "as is" really *is* bad!

The "Bad" Case of Ron and Selena

Ron's wife, Selena, was beautiful, exceptionally bright, and also a "terror." Selena continually screamed at their two-year-old daughter, Doris, refused to follow her doctor's suggestions for her present pregnancy, and told everyone — especially Ron himself — what a rotten husband, father, and store manager Ron was. Apologize? Never! Respond to Ron sexually? Rarely. Admit that she was disturbed? Of course not!

Selena acknowledged most of Ron's complaints during their couple counseling sessions, but insisted that he was even worse than she was. Twice a week he stayed up almost all night, playing poker with the boys. He neglected his work so badly that he had been fired four times in five years. He did practically nothing around the house. Ron acknowledged these delinquencies, but claimed that he had been a "prince" with his previous wife, and only behaved the way he now did because Selena was such a "sexless bitch." Al hoped their admissions were a breakthrough:

No go. Both Ron and Selena insisted — and I mean *insisted* — that the other's behavior was unforgivable, and that his or her "as is" *had* to change before each would work on their own behavior. Even little changes — such as Selena not castigating Ron in front of others, and Ron helping slightly with household chores — were angrily resisted. "You first, partner, then I'll change!"

I thought of recommending a quiet — and almost friendly — divorce. But, to my surprise, they would have none of it. Ron insisted that he *really* loved Selena — despite all. Selena couldn't *think* of breaking up a family that soon was about to include a second child.

Back to the impasse. Neither would even think of trying to change "as is" until the other did. Their only good choice would be to follow the philosophy of acceptance of Reinhold Niebuhr and REBT: "Give me the courage to change what I can change, the serenity to accept what I cannot change, and the wisdom to know the difference." Fine, but how could I get Ron and Selena to follow this wise plan?

I pummeled away at several of the absolutistic musts that both of them held:

• "My partner is wrong and absolutely must not be the way she is."
• "My mate must change first and reward me before I can change."
• "Anyone would be — and must be — incensed by my partner. Being furious is the only way to react to this kind of horror!"
• "If I forgive my mate, as I shouldn't have to, I would be a sniveling weakling, and not at all my good self!"
• "Acting nasty the way I do to my partner will finally get me somewhere. So I must persist in vicious fighting."
• "If I make my mate feel guilty and show him what a perfect louse he is, that will help bring about the change I want!"

I finally was able to help Selena and Ron by showing them how to actively dispute these *musts* and turn them back into *preferences*. They partly began to accept "as is" with each other. I employed another REBT technique, getting them to role-play *each other*, rigidly holding on to the other's demands, while forcefully trying to talk each other out of them. Thus, Ron rigidly held on to Selena's belief that she had to have two-year-old Doris always obey her and *must* drill perfect obediency into the child. Selena did her best to talk him out of this (her own) idea. In doing so, she finally saw how ridiculous the idea was. In fact, a day after their role-play in my office, Selena burst out laughing while she was severely castigating Doris for not listening to her, and thereafter dramatically reduced the screaming at their daughter.

It took several months, but Ron began to accept much of Selena's obnoxious behavior "as is." Selena also accepted her daughter's "horrible" behavior, and was much more accepting of some of Ron's. I can't honestly say that Ron and Selena lived happily ever after as a result of my marriage counseling. But they both began to see that the other's "as is" behavior, however "wrong" it might be, still was realistically part of their marital reality. That helped them a lot. [AE]

Try This At Home!

You may not be as extreme as Ron and Selena, so here is a simple exercise to try when you are upset:

- Is what I'm saying or believing 100% true? (Example: "Does my partner *always* contradict me? *Often? Once in a while?*")
- What is the worst that realistically can happen? (Example: "If he or she often contradicts me, I'll just have to go to the trouble of ignoring it or of talking back uselessly.")
- What are the disadvantages in my upsetting myself about various situations? (Example: "I'll make myself anxious and bring on more contradictions by him or her. I'll get a pain in my gut and other possible psychosomatic reactions.")
- What are some advantages in this same situation? (Example: "I could go out of my way to see her good points. I could gain control over my self-created anger.")
- Do I choose to focus on the advantages or on the disadvantages? (Example: "The advantages of learning what I may have done wrong, and controlling my anger even if I wasn't wrong.") If you are only mildly upset, try rewording your *should* or *must* to the phrase, "It would be better if..."

When you are emotionally involved in a relationship situation, it's hard to distinguish between *rationality* and *irrationality*. Here is an easy distinction: Rationality accepts social reality "as it is"; irrationality demands that reality *should* and *must* be different than "it is."

Guideline 1 can be quite difficult. Keep working at it as we move on to Guideline 2 in the next chapter.

6

Guideline 2:
Express Appreciation Frequently

*Express appreciation frequently. Avoid steady criticism. Acknowledge
your partner often for small things. Find, discover, or even create
things you really value about your partner. Say them. Honesty is
important here. Avoid the main relationship "killer" — frequent
criticism of your partner.*

An especially easy way to influence others is by expressing
honest appreciation. What makes it easy? You simply replace
criticism of your partner with honest appreciation. Does this
usually work? Yes, indeed. Most people respond positively to
honest appreciation, and negatively to criticism. The famed
psychiatrist Alfred Adler noted that most people don't just want or
desire appreciation, but actually *crave* it.

For example, when Selena (mentioned in our last chapter)
screamed at her two-year-old daughter, it "made" her husband Tad
very angry. At first he lambasted her for "abusing" that "poor two-
year-old who can hardly help herself." He benefited from his REBT
sessions when he realized, although Selena was "wrong," he *chose*
to make himself enraged at her. As he grew in awareness of what
was happening, he gave up much of his anger and replaced it with
healthy feelings of sorrow and disappointment. When Selena
continued screaming at their daughter, he was able to say, "I'm
really glad that you pay so much attention to Doris and respect her
ability to change." Stopped in her tracks by Tad's unusual
appreciation of her behavior, Selena ceased her screaming at Doris,
and saw the virtue of what she was doing — observing Doris's
behavior — and began to plan how to help Doris behave better.

This easy way to influence others is stated in Guideline 2. You may wish to use the short version of this guideline, making it easier to remember:

Express appreciation frequently. Avoid steady criticism.

Some Discoveries About Appreciation

Here are several important discoveries Ted made when he first started using this guideline with his wife, Jolanta:

First, I had assumed that she was more often wrong than right. I discovered that she was more often right than wrong. My assumption was mistaken.

Second, when I would tell Jolanta how often she was right, she would disagree. "No, Ted, it is not I who am so often right, it is you who are often right." She was right about me, but mistaken about herself. I discovered that I am more often right than wrong also. In time we together discovered that both of us are more often right than wrong. This is another example of "and/also" instead of "either/or."

Third, now I was curious about people in general. And all of the people I looked at also seemed to be more often right than wrong. That was another significant discovery for me. [TC]

You can train yourself to look carefully to find things that your partner is doing "right," and to clearly and fully express your appreciation for those "good" things. This idea is presented particularly well in the book, *The One Minute Manager*. With some practice, you will usually find that this becomes easy, satisfying, and fun to do. Yes, you can catch your partner doing something right!

One of our clients is so delighted with this guideline that she practices giving appreciation to her two pet birds. She says she feels uplifted when she does it. Whether or not you are a bird lover, try "giving appreciation" to others.

Giving your partner appreciation often becomes a pleasure in itself. What usually happens when you criticize, is that your partner goes on guard and becomes defensive, moving away from easy-flowing communication exchange, and perhaps shifting into a turbulent argument. When you give honest appreciation, your partner tends to relax and become more open to exploring your point of view.

When Tad went out of his way to show his wife honest appreciation for some of her "wrong" screaming at their daughter, and when he pointed out to Selena his appreciation for the "good" attention she was giving Doris, Selena began to respond much better to Tad *and* Doris. It took Tad a few expressions of appreciations of this sort to make things with Selena work. But his appreciation paid off much better than his previous criticism!

Ted also confirms what Al claimed many years ago. That is, the *types of mistakes* people make are few in number, but — unfortunately — frequently repeated. These mistakes may be summed up as "shoulding and "demanding," confusing your opinion with the absolute "truth," overgeneralizing, and globally rating yourself and other people.

Some Ways To Find Things To Appreciate

Almost every situation has both advantages and disadvantages. You can choose to look for the advantages or the disadvantages. Too often, people seem to choose to look for the disadvantages. Instead, if you choose to focus on the advantage, no matter how small it may seem to be, this advantage can serve as a base for giving appreciation.

If your partner was in an auto accident and wasn't injured, that is an advantage to appreciate, "What is more important to me than the money or the car is that you are uninjured." If your partner cries and feels ashamed for causing the accident, you can acknowledge that your partner made a mistake, even made a serious mistake, and then say, "Thank God you are not perfect. You are human like me. I make mistakes too. I wouldn't know what to do with you if you were perfect." Al likes this example from one of his clients:

Joe foolishly participated in a high-stakes poker game and lost five hundred dollars, which he and his wife Marge could ill afford. First she was furious and on the verge of bawling him out and buying a fur coat to punish him further. When Guideline 2 was explained to her, she began to stop making herself angry and gave Joe appreciation by saying, "Now we can't afford that Bermuda vacation we planned, so I don't have to worry about the risk of scuba diving. I really can thank you for that." She thought that was a feeble kind of appreciation, but it worked, because Joe appreciated her not bawling him out. [AE]

Flowing and Interjecting

Go with the flow. Interject comments when your partner makes a point you agree with, or that you like it. "You're right." "That's a good point." "You said that beautifully." "That was eloquently stated." "How well you worded it." "I like that." "Oh, that felt good."

Honesty is a key part of this guideline, of course. If you give appreciation *too* frequently, your partner may realize this is a "technique," question your honesty, and reject the comment altogether.

You may choose to listen without interjecting, then make some comments of your own. If so, support and appreciate your partner with something you honestly agree with before you state your difference, or disagreement. "I want to give you some support for your position before I share my possible difference." "I like your view on... but I differ with your emphasis..." "I like that idea, but I see it a little differently..." Use your own words to fit your specific situation.

If you feel hurt, resentful, or angry, and you choose the REBT responsibility for mastering your feelings, you might say something like this: "You provide me with the opportunity to work on what I'm telling myself for improving my emotional growth."

And, of course, there are the old standbys of saying, "Thank you," and "I appreciate..." "Thank you for sharing," or "I appreciate your contribution to my understanding."

Appreciation may be retroactive, too. "Yesterday, what you said left me so angry, but after I thought about it, I decided you were right. Thanks for jarring me out of my rut."

Caring Communication

Criticism makes the "easy" more difficult and complex. Avoiding criticism is everyone's desire, and yet criticizing is what almost everyone does! Who does not find disapproval dictatorial and painful? Damned few! Most of us respond to it by defensively protecting ourselves and attacking our accuser. We tend to distance ourselves — or stay and fight like hell. Yes, we may even resort to physical violence. At best these relationships break up and end in divorce; at worst, they dramatically continue! Criticism usually combines two elements: (1) correcting the other, and (2) blaming the other. Blaming is what makes the criticism destructive.

Constructive Criticism Is Not Blaming

Don't confuse constructive criticism and blaming. Criticism — as in "constructive criticism" — is correcting the other without blaming for mistakes made. Blaming is demanding that the other change, plus condemning the other for the mistake(s). Constructive criticism may sometimes help improve a situation, while blaming usually adds an emotional burden — making an unwanted situation worse.

Marge, who surrendered her anger at her husband for losing five-hundred dollars in high-stakes poker, first thought, "How could you do a stupid thing like that? We really needed that money and you *shouldn't* impulsively risk playing that kind of poker game!" She thought this was constructive criticism because it would show Joe that (1) he was acting stupidly, (2) they could have used the five-hundred dollars he lost, and (3) he *preferably* should resist the temptation of a high-stakes game. When she made herself "unangry" at Joe, she saw that he would take her "constructive" criticism very badly, even though it was factually accurate. So she reduced her anger and potential blaming, and constructively gave appreciation to Joe for saving her from the scuba diving that she considered dangerous. Later she had a calm discussion with him and pointed out the factual disadvantages of his gambling.

On the other hand, criticism *may* occasionally add credibility, some excitement, and may even present an interesting angle to a relationship, making the relationship feel more "satisfying." Use *occasional* criticism sparingly — and constructively.

Let us look again at our suggestion for Guideline 2:

Express appreciation frequently. Avoid steady criticism.

Acknowledge your partner for small things. Find, discover, or even create things you really value about your partner. Say them.

Honesty is important here. Avoid the main relationship "killer" — frequent criticism.

Immediacy of reinforcement and the schedule of reinforcement are the keys. The *quantity* of your appreciations will be more important and more valued than the importance or "size" of what you appreciated. Therefore we use the word "frequently." It is also important to note that you can overdo the frequency and "spoil" the good effect.

Replacing Criticism With Appreciation

We know what you're thinking. "*How* do I replace criticism with appreciation?" First, by changing your attitude about being criticized yourself. Many people really resist this one. When your partner is critical of you, assume that her intention is to help and not harm you. See the criticism in a benign frame — as a *difference*, not a *battle* between the two of you. Ted's wife Jolanta recommends this reframing because it feels so good when he uses it with her.

On one particular occasion when Jolanta was berating me for not fully understanding her, I thought about defensively "proving" that I really did understand her, and that she did not understand me. But I stopped myself by realizing that she was actually implementing open communication by expressing her anger. So I thanked her for sharing her feelings and pointed out that that was a fine contribution to our communication and to our marriage.

Jolanta was surprised. "Why do you like my expression of anger?" she wanted to know. She had expected me to dislike it and to fight back. "Because," I said, "your anger belongs in our communication, just because it is there — like Mount Everest was there for Sir Edmund Hillary. Whether I like it or not, it is part of our situation. Your anger is something for *us* to learn to deal with." Jolanta's original outrage showed me where she was emotionally. I found this to be invaluable. It helped alert me to things I do about which she upsets herself. If I openly — without anger — accept this information, I can probably relate better to her in the future. So, the information conveyed by her anger was good, even though I might not know exactly how I would put it to good use until later.

Discovering something to appreciate often involves *creating* something to appreciate. What I objected to was Jolanta's way of expressing her rage, rather than the fact of its existence. She was blaming, accusatory, and demanding, and she was self-righteously assuming that I had no justification for my side at all! Only *her* position seemed valid to her. Emotionally, she had no room for my differing point of view. As noted above, I mainly wanted a way of communicating that allowed us to share our differences and disagreements successfully. At first, she didn't allow that at all. But by implementing Guidelines 1 and 2, I used her anger as an opportunity to ward off my own anger, and to create a more collaborative, non-demanding approach to our communication. [TC]

When Differences Make a Difference

Differences are natural because they naturally do exist. Just as a difference in height between two people is natural, a difference in thoughts, feelings, and behavior is also "normal" and "natural." When your partner criticizes you, and you do not agree with the criticism, accept — rather than oppose — the fact that you differ. Yes, indeed you differ — what two people do not? Free yourself of your rancor about your obvious differences, accept the fact that differences will always exist, and then it will be easy to find and share good things about your mate.

Stop stabbing yourself with the knife of your partner's criticism — and stop stabbing her back about it! Reframe criticism as a constructive suggestion — even if not constructively presented — for you and your partner to consider. Put aside your vulnerable ego, ignore any deprecating tone, and think about the beneficial suggestions that may be included — and perhaps hidden — in the criticism's angry tone. If you *honestly* find the "suggestion" a good one, say so. If you don't like the "suggestion," thank your partner for his or her good intentions to improve your relationship.

Even carping criticism may include a good idea, or at least the spark of a good idea. If you see it this way, a negative remark may still serve as a springboard between you and your partner. Just the acknowledgment of your mate's good intentions can soothe bad feelings and help him become more receptive to your own suggestions.

Suppose that you see your partner's criticism as an arrogant demand. A demand that you change your ways! What then? If you are wise, you can still reframe this demand as a *proposal,* look to find the "good idea" that may be hidden in the demand, then relate to the "good idea" as a *possibility* to consider. However blastingly it is presented, think of it as a suggestion that you can choose to take — or to acknowledge without anger, and ultimately to ignore.

When you feel critical of your partner, acknowledge again that you may have a *difference* with her, rather than *blaming* your partner. Then discuss and plan how the two of you may possibly deal with that difference.

How can you first change your own response when you feel quite critical? Observe that, along with your sharp criticism, you usually have hostile feelings. These stem from your underlying demandingness, such as, "My partner doesn't understand me as he *should*!" "My partner doesn't agree with me or support me as she *must*!"

These self-statements, of course, are silly and self-defeating. If you and I are talking, why *must* you understand my meaning my way? Answer: No reason at all. Where is it written that you *should* agree with me? Answer: Only in my nutty head! Actually, you will understand my meaning *your* way — because you can only go by *your* learning and *your* experiences when trying to make sense out of my message.

Here again, it is useful to distinguish between *must* and *desirability*. From my point of view, it is highly *desirable* that you understand my meaning my way, but there is no reason why you *must* do what I find desirable. Almost everyone does something that is not desirable, such as smoking, eating or drinking too much, procrastinating, or blaming others. You are still a normal human being, even when you don't do what I deem desirable. If I now work at accepting *you* more fully, I may be able to figure out a way to help you understand *my* meaning better.

Even if you do understand my meaning, that doesn't mean that you must agree with me. You can understand almost everything I say — and agree with very little of it. Thus, you can understand that I believe in Zeus without either agreeing or disagreeing with me. Similarly, you can nicely distinguish between understanding another, and agreeing or disagreeing with him if you choose to!

Returning to the problem of you and I having a serious disagreement and my commanding that you *absolutely must* agree with my views. Why must you? No reason. Like me, you always have the right to be wrong.

So, even if I'm right, there is no reason why you *must* agree with me. If it were true that you *had to* agree with me, you would automatically do what you obviously had to do — agree. Because you clearly don't agree with me, my idea that you *must* do so is obviously unrealistic. I'd better accept what exists — which is that you don't agree with my view. Now, let me figure out what I can sensibly choose to do about our disagreements.

Back again, to you and your partner. When you angrily criticize her, you very likely make an effort to see that your criticism, however worded, really consists of (1) an implied statement of a difference that you have with her, and (2) a demanding protest that she *should not, must not* differ with a noble person like yourself! In other words, you're reacting to an existing difference that you don't like, and demanding that the difference *must not* exist! These are contradictory perceptions. Do your best to see *both* her *difference with* you and your *protest against* her having this difference. Strive to accept — instead of railing against — this natural difference. You may have little choice of noticing how different the two of you are. But you can choose, or not choose, to deal sensibly with this difference.

Anger Over Smoking

Lots of people these days make themselves very angry at their partner's smoking because, they insist, it is potentially lethal, it is offensive, it turns off many people, it is inconsiderate, it is expensive, etc., etc., etc. Al has many such folks among his clients:

> I show them that it is very easy to argue against the undesirability and disadvantages of their partner's smoking. But it still doesn't mean that he *absolutely must* stop his very *undesirable* behavior. Stopping smoking is *greatly desirable* — perhaps even life-saving — but not *absolutely necessary*. I finally help *most* of these nonsmokers give up their rage at their smoking partners, but not all! Some of them are just as insistent that their mates stop smoking as their mates are demanding to continue to smoke. Two screwballs — or, more accurately, two people who act screwballishly much of the time — and a fairly crummy partnership! [AE]

Good Intentions May Be Seen As Criticism

Returning to Guideline 2 and the advice, "Express appreciation frequently." This is not exactly the usual human condition! Most people seem more ready to criticize than to appreciate. Their "good intention" to help their partner is often seen as an "unfair attack" that needs to be defended against. Then the emotional distance between the partners grows larger.

In your own case, you may have noticed that your sharp — and frequent — criticism tends to trigger woeful antagonisms. Your partner may well see it as an unloving and uncalled-for intention to control, or as a demand for perfection that violates his right to be a fallible, imperfect human. Reacting to this "unfair" attack, he may weakly conform to your demands, and hate you and himself for being "cowardly." Or, of course, he may become stubbornly rebellious and *increase* the behavior you hate — just to show you that you are indubitably wrong, wrong, wrong. Your criticism thus works wonders to "inspire" more of what you *don't* want — greater bickering and fighting!

Actually, criticism is usually unnecessary, because if you want to help your partner change, there are noncritical ways for you to do this. We will cover better alternatives to criticism when we get to Guidelines 3 and 4.

Note again that we have not said "never criticize." Our more realistic message is "seldom criticize." Instead, *frequently* appreciate your partner — especially in small things.

Consider our illustration of Frank and Francis again, and look at Frank's self-defeating *must*: "I must be honest with Frances and get her to stop and to think carefully — as, of course, she *should* do! — before she opens her stupid mouth!" He then blasted her with his "honest" and "correct" opinion. Though he often had "the best intentions," she heard his "worst" ones. The message she received ("I can't do anything right!"), was *not* the message he wanted to send! Criticizing your partner, however good your intentions are, can be quite a dangerous tactic. Watch it! Think it through before you speak.

After Frank began to feel comfortable with Guideline 1, he found Guideline 2 surprisingly easy. Before he succeeded in accepting Frances "*as is*," he found very little to appreciate about her. When she made a suggestion that he didn't like, he quickly responded with, "That's a stupid idea!" As you can imagine, that observation went over like the proverbial "lead balloon." Frank mistakenly believed, "I *must* be honest with Frances and get her to stop and think before she acts so stupidly!" Instead, she usually concluded, "He doesn't respect my opinion, or respect *me*. I hate it when he puts me down! I *can't stand it*! I've *got* to get out of this marriage! I can't please him, as I *have* to do! If I stay, I'm a weakling!" So, instead of considering that her suggestion to Frank may have had flaws, she angrily felt that she *had to* uphold it and "prove" that it was valid.

After following Guideline 1, accepting Frances "as she is," Frank saw the value of Guideline 2, and would sometimes diplomatically ask, "Are you sure that is what you want me to do?" Frances would pause, do some thinking out loud, and usually come to agree with him on her own, without his having said anything more. In this new context, Frank was easily able to give Frances some honest appreciation for how intelligent she was. When he did this, she felt respected, and he felt good in his relationship with her. He started to tell himself, as well as other people, "You know, I have a very intelligent wife." He now found many things to appreciate about Frances, and took pride in many of her actions.

Like Frank, you can invent your own way to show appreciation to your partner. You may borrow from this book, from other sources, and from your own ingenuity.

When Frank used Rational Emotive Behavior Therapy and the first two communication guidelines, he helped his wife feel appreciated, rather than criticized, and she often started to move toward his position. Surprisingly, people usually move *toward* your position when you are sincerely interested in exploring theirs. Why? Because your interest in their position creates more trust of the value of your opinion. They may not *adopt* your position, but they are more likely to move in your direction. You thereby, non-coercively and positively, influence them.

There Almost Always Is Some Little Thing To Appreciate
Guideline 2 includes: "Find, discover, or even create things you really value about your partner." You can help yourself do this by looking for some *advantage* in what your partner says and does — no matter how "wrong" or "bad" you at first find the statement or action to be. Even if the advantage you discover is small, emphasize it. Every situation has both advantages and disadvantages. Look for the disadvantages in "wrong" behavior, but *choose* to focus on its advantages, however small they may be.

Ted describes his first year of marriage with Jolanta:
She would sometimes get angry, or even furious, with me. I did not want, like, nor enjoy her anger, and my first inner response was defensive and self-justifying. "When I haven't done anything wrong, she *should not* act that way to an innocent soul like me!" Nonetheless, following Guideline 2, I was determined to find an honest response that would leave her with a win.

I put aside my first possible response, which was, "There is no reason for you to make yourself so angry at me, sweetheart. I can't see that I have behaved that badly." Instead, I looked for one of Jolanta's good points to appreciate as an alternative response. For instance, "You may well be right about what you are telling me to do. You are usually very perceptive about my mistakes." And then I elaborated on the good points I found. I chose this kind of positive response instead of the first negative one that I felt like saying.

Usually, I could find a positive response almost immediately. But occasionally I would take several days to find something to appreciate about Jolanta's comments. After such a delay, I again brought up the situation that she was angry over and shared my comforting appreciation of her. As time went on I became more skillful in finding things to appreciate, brought them up sooner, and Jolanta became much less hostile. Clearly, I began to influence her to be more receptive to my positions.

Once I overcame the unexpected shock of Jolanta's angry attack and accepted her "as is" — instead of blaming her for being that "rotten" way — I could concentrate on giving her appreciation. "I don't want us to hide things from each other." By reminding myself how much I desired open communication, I was able to push myself to discover something about Jolanta's behavior to appreciate.

Keep in mind that the third and fourth sentences of Communication Guideline 2 ("Find, discover, or even create things you really value about your partner") are, "Say them" and "Honesty is important here."

When words of appreciation honestly occur to you, saying them may sometimes seem inappropriate. Be brief and say them anyway. You add to the frequency of your appreciation. And if it is a surprise, fine! [TC]

Distinguishing Between Appreciation and Flattery

Honest appreciation is saying something good or nice about a person that is accurate. The individual has done something, and you mention what was done and that you find it good. *Flattery* is when you exaggerate the goodness of what they have done or exaggerate how "great" the individual is for having done it.

Ben was a client of Al's who tried flattery when he felt guilty. On the day he bought an expensive lunch for his friend, Ed, he didn't tell his wife, Martha. Instead, he deliberately looked for things to flatter her about. On the same day he indulged in the expensive lunch, he found Martha's haircut "ravishing" — it was just her usual style. He effusively thanked her for getting it cut and said that it would make a "marvelous" impression on the friends they were seeing the next evening. He also found that night's meal — which she had quickly thrown together — "scrumptious and unbeatable." Martha liked his flattery at first, but was suspicious. Eventually he confessed to treating Ed to a very expensive lunch.

Don't mix your honesty with crass flattery. Flattery is — and usually shows itself to be — insincere. Honesty is much better, especially when your honest appreciation is for something specific. Instead of using vague flattery like, "You are wonderful," be more specific: "I enjoy your sincere passion when you express yourself." (Assuming, of course, that you honestly *do* enjoy your partner's passion.)

The last sentence of Guideline 2, you'll recall, is, "Avoid the main relationship killer — frequent criticism of your partner." This leads us to the important question of what else you might do instead of criticizing your partner — in addition to appreciation. The guidelines ahead help answer this question.

7

Guideline 3:
Communicate From Integrity

How To Make Honesty Work For You

Communicate from integrity: Be honest regarding beliefs and evidence that conflict with your own views of what is happening. When your partner is right, admit it. Be both honest and tactful. Allow different perceptions to exist. Agree to stop penalizing each other for your honesty as you now often may do. Agree that both of you will be honest and let the other "get away" with honesty.

Just before writing this chapter Ted had an unexpected visit with an old friend.

"You taught me how to be honest," he told me. "How did I do that?" I asked in surprise. He pulled out his copy of these guidelines and pointed to Guideline 3. This was the first time in ten years that he had said anything about the Seven Guidelines. He liked this guideline and chose to work at becoming more artfully honest. Using the third guideline he claimed he now assertively goes after what he wants, and he affirms himself without embarrassment. Instead of assuming the role of false modesty, as before, he now readily and delightedly acknowledges how good he thinks he is. In effect he applies the view of George Bernard Shaw, "I think I'm good, so why not admit it." He feels more emotionally free. [TC]

Most forms of psychotherapy advocate honesty, particularly being honest about your own thoughts and feelings. Who are you if you pretend that you don't feel what you do feel, and if you "do feel" what you don't experience? Certainly not yourself! Our view is similar to Shakespeare's "To thine own self be true," and to the AA's step: "And when we were wrong, promptly admitted it."

How can you feel what you don't experience? Damned clever! The answer is "easily" with a should. If you feel sad, but you should feel happy, you fake it by presenting a happy countenance.

Many Therapies Sneak In "Shoulds" And "Musts"

Many psychotherapies, however, are themselves dishonest in that they sneak in their own *shoulds* and *musts* that interfere with helping clients to see and reduce their self- and other-demandingness. Al saw this when he was being supervised as a therapist at Columbia University in their clinical psychology program:

Donald, a sixteen-year-old boy, was a client. Donald had just about a 100 I.Q., but came from a highly intelligent and achieving family. His mother, father, uncles, and aunts all thought he should do outstandingly well in his courses, and he strongly agreed with them. Result: despite his hard work in high school (in the privileged community of Scarsdale, New York), he rarely finished a course with a B or better, almost always got Cs, and kept failing at math. Obviously, NO chance for Harvard! Donald was severely depressed.

I could quickly see that Donald, along with his close relatives, had unrealistic academic goals, and that I'd better help him settle for lesser aspirations — perhaps as an auto mechanic like he very much wanted to be.

Unfortunately, Columbia's clinical psychology department at that time was highly addicted to Carl Rogers and his nondirective therapy, especially my supervisor. I couldn't very well easily dissuade Donald, not to mention his parents, of his high-flung academic ambitions. Indirectly asking him how he felt about his goals and about dismally failing at them got both of us nowhere. After vainly trying Rogerian non-directive therapy with Donald for several sessions and seeing him make himself dangerously self-hating and suicidal, I became much more direct with him. I praised his adeptness at fixing cars and playing soccer, and showed him that he didn't have to get good marks and become an accountant or a lawyer. I pushed him to thinking for himself, instead of killing himself to endorse his family's views about achievement.

Fine! After another month of seeing Donald, and one session of honestly telling his parents the facts of life, I helped him to transfer to a trade school the next term, be unashamed and undepressed, and enthusiastically start preparing for classes in mechanics. Even my supervisor was highly pleased with these results, but I partially led him to believe that I had achieved them by counseling Donald non-directively. After I got my Ph.D. from Columbia, I told my supervisor the whole truth, and even helped wean him away somewhat from his own Rogerian non-directive practice.

A near repetition of this incident happened almost a decade later when I had become a psychoanalyst. I was again rather passively exploring the dire need of a 27-year-old dentist, Marion, to be loved. *Professionally,* she was quite honest with her patients, firmly told them what procedures had to be done with their teeth and gums, and rigorously kept after them to do their dental homework. Some of her patients objected to her noncoddling demeanor, and left her for more kindly and gentle practitioners. Did she therefore reform her rigorous ways? Not a bit!

Oddly enough, Marion was a *social* basket case. She needed, or thought she needed, the love and affection of her parents, her husband, her friends, and, well, you name it. She rarely had social thoughts, feelings, or actions of her own, and became a love slob who turned herself into an affable chameleon.

I kept proceeding psychoanalytically to show Marion how, as a child, she "needed" to win her mother away from her obsession with Marion's father; how she "had to" win her sister's love to compensate for not being as pretty as her sister was; and how she was "compelled" to get approval from other boys and girls because she felt she wasn't as bright as they were, and thought they would abandon her. Marion was able to clearly see these reasons for her "love-slob" style, but this insight, as is often the case in psychoanalysis, didn't help her to stop behaving as a chameleon. She still feared trying to honestly be herself.

Since psychoanalytic insight wasn't working, I again risked being quite directive and philosophical. I spent several weeks showing Marion the great disadvantages of selling her soul for approval. I strongly disputed her Irrational Beliefs, (IBs), that she would be entirely alone if she showed others what she really thought and felt. I admitted that being loved by others was great, but that caring for herself independently could be much more freeing and less anxiety provoking. I had her agree to take homework assignments, to refuse to do some of her parents' bidding, and to keep seeing friends that her husband did not want her to see.

What do you know? My active-directive methods soon worked much better with Marion than my more passive psychoanalytic methods had been working. Within the next two months she began to be almost as assertive and firm with her friends and relatives as she had been with patients in her dental practice. Yes, she did lose a few of her friends who still demanded subservience, but only a few. And for the first time in her nonprofessional life she began to befriend herself. She gave up her love-slobism, liked her new assertive style, and felt immensely free to be herself.

Marion and I also found, somewhat to our own surprise, that her relationship with her husband actually improved as she honestly acknowledged some real disagreements with him, and as she held her ground by seeing some women friends to whom he objected. At first, Jerry was somewhat hostile and withdrawn about her new assertiveness. But he then realized that, in return for Marion dishonestly shutting her mouth about her disagreements with him, and pretending that she always liked doing things his way, he too had been walking on eggshells, hiding some of his own wishes. Jerry wanted especially to be friendly with his ex-girlfriend, Liz. He had given up that friendship when he first began the relationship with Marion, and had never permitted himself to have a heart-to-heart talk with Liz since that time. Now that Marion was honestly being herself and he saw that he could accept this, he realized that she could probably also handle his being more his honest self. So he tried that, including a few dinner dates with Liz, and it worked. He and Marion were then both able to open up more with each other, and at the same time open up more within themselves.

As a result of my work with Marion and several other clients with whom I started to be more active-directive, I abandoned calling myself a psychoanalyst by the beginning of 1953, and I started experimenting more and doing heavy research into other therapy techniques. By January of 1955, I was well on the road to creating REBT! [AE]

Ted Tells a Tale of Honesty, Too

Complete honesty is a tough standard to live up to, as Ted learned from experience:

> One day, some time before I learned about REBT, I decided to experiment with complete honesty all day long. That intention lasted until about noon. A friend proudly showed me his newly painted kitchen. I didn't like either the color or the paint job, but I didn't have the heart to tell him so. I didn't want to disappoint him, so I told him a white lie.
>
> I learned from this experience that 100% honesty is not always the best policy, because sometimes I want to show respect for other's feelings, rather than "fix" them according to my "honest" view of things.
>
> I also had the curious and uncomfortable experience of feeling like a five-year-old while I forced myself to focus on 100% honest responses to others. When I stopped my experiment with honesty at noontime, I again had the more comfortable experience of feeling like an adult.
>
> On thinking over this experience, I decided that honesty takes more skill than I had, and that I could choose to learn those additional skills, whatever they might turn out to be. When people are angry or hostile, usually they are also mistaken to some small or large degree. While angry, they typically dogmatically deny any possibility of being mistaken. In Guideline 3, the most important skill to learn is: Honestly accept beliefs and evidence that conflict with your own views of what is happening or is factual and then revise your position accordingly.
>
> Do this with even small things, as in the following illustration: I called a friend and the phone rang without an answer. "Oh," I thought, "No one is home." Then I thought about my thought. "I don't really *know* that no one is home. All I know for sure is that no one answered the phone. My friend might be in the bathroom and not available, or he might be in the backyard and not hear the phone."
>
> Using my example of the phone, I began changing my opinionated statements of dogmatic "certainty" to more tentative possibilities. I then realized that my life had more creative possibilities than I had imagined. To my surprise, my creativity expanded. I became significantly more open to my possible mistakes, and to the differences and disagreements of others. [TC]

Shoulds And Musts Require Dishonesty

Ted's next adventure with honesty came with exploring Rational Emotive Behavior Therapy.

When I let go of my *shoulds* and *musts,* honesty got easier. Much easier! Sometimes I offer to go to the store. Wanting to protect my time, Jolanta often says, "Ted, you don't have to go to the store. I can go." I agree with her, "You're right. I don't *have* to go. I *choose* to go." Previous to learning about *shoulds* and *musts,* I would argue the point, "Yes, I do *have* to go because...." But now we may discuss it briefly, since either one of us can go. Sometimes we agree for me to go; sometimes we agree for her to go; sometimes we agree to go together. Without the *shoulds* and *have to's* (another phrase for musts), it is a pleasant conversation, not a hassle. A seemingly small change in our way of talk, but such a big difference in how we communicate. [TC]

Connecting With Feelings

While exploring my feelings and the beliefs behind them, I gained more contact with my feelings, something I had significantly lost in my late teens. Feelings confused me until I learned that my confusion centered around "shoulds" and "musts." I realized that I "should" feel what, in fact, I often did not feel. For example, that I should feel sad or sorry when I did not feel sad nor sorry. I should feel competent when I actually felt inadequate. I had taught myself to pretend having these feelings because it seemed the "safe" or the "right" thing to do socially.

As I continue to explore shoulds and musts, I have come to discover that these demands require some degree of dishonesty. Shoulds and musts often require pretending about what is not so, and hiding what is so. The combination of pretending and hiding is a basic pattern of neurotic responses.

As I used REBT to change my musts back into preferences, I could actually feel my feelings, instead of pretending to feel them. I could feel sorry when I was sorry or glad when I felt glad. Most of the time I didn't have to hide what I really felt, and could readily share my real feelings with others. Nor did I have to compulsively "share" or hide my differences or disagreements. With compulsion there is no experience of choice. However, with REBT I learned I really did have the choice to express or not to express what I was feeling. I began to look for that choice, and to find it.

Choosing to give up your musts and to feel your honest feelings takes practice. In time, REBT showed me a clear link between my thoughts and feelings. This link, in turn, enabled me to connect better with the thoughts and feelings of others. It also enabled me to confront my own fear of sharing differences and disagreements. [TC]

Al's Example of Bart and Marie

Ted's trouble with being honest with himself when he holds to his musts is repeated by many of my clients. For example, Bart believed that he must at all times strongly love his wife, Marie, even when she acted nastily to him. So he lied to himself that her nastiness was intriguing, and he lied to Marie that it didn't bother him at all. When she meanly made him a poor meal because he "deserved it" for not being attentive enough to her, he saw her as a "cute" child and pretended to enjoy the food. Marie believed that he always *should* attend to her fully and completely, and saw deliberately depriving Bart of her usually well-prepared meal as a good act, because it taught that inattentive bastard a well-deserved lesson and properly trained him to be more considerate.

When I helped Bart see his need to always act lovingly toward Marie, even when she was quite nasty, he changed this need to a preference, honestly admitted to himself that he briefly hated her at such times, and now would refuse to eat the rotten meal she had deliberately foisted on him. He just remarked, That's far below your regular cooking, dear. Maybe I'll have something later."

When he first did this, Marie made herself angrier and nastier than ever, and responded, "Oh, lost your appetite, did you? Well, you deserve to, considering how much you have been ignoring me!" That, of course, got her less attention than ever, as Bart went to his reading and later made himself a snack.

When I helped Marie see her *dire need* — in addition to her normal desire — for Bart's full attention, she at first resisted changing it, and stoutly held that it was normal and that all wives had it. "Maybe so," I replied. "But where does it get them when their husbands are not attentive?" "Nowhere," she finally realized, and began to change her *need* to a strong *preference*. She reversed her attitude and behavior, and when Bart was preoccupied with his own affairs and inattentive to her, she forced herself to be nicer than usual to him, make him an unusually good meal, and tell him some of her own problems that had nothing to do with him. As you can guess, that often (though not always) worked.

Both Bart and Marie reduced their demands, were much more honest with themselves and with each other, and got more of what they wanted from their relationship. [AE]

When your partner "confesses" to something you don't like, make a point to appreciate your partner's honesty, instead of punishing him. Keep in mind that what you have with your partner really is a difference or a disagreement, and treat it as such. Seriously work at applying this part of the third guideline: Agree to stop penalizing each other for your honesty, as you now often may do. Agree that you both will be honest, and let the other "get away" with honesty.

We will look at sharing differences and disagreements in the next chapter.

8

Guideline 4:
Share and Explore Differences
With Your Partner

How To Move Toward A Win-Win

*Share and explore differences with your partner. Explore
disagreements with your partner to move toward a win-win
outcome, a higher resolution that accepts parts of both your views.
Or, to agree to disagree. Additionally, be ready to compromise
without pretending that you agree when you really don't agree.*

A conflict with another individual exists when the two of you
have opposing values. We move toward a win-win when the
differences in our opposing values are successfully shared. We
may create a win-win when we together successfully accept the
differences in our opposing values.

Few people are willing to follow Peace Pilgrim's ideal of the
Golden Rule for resolving conflicts: "Have as your objective the
resolving of the conflict, and not the gaining of advantage." For
those who choose, this is a simple, workable approach. However,
for most people, the gaining of advantage is their objective, which
seems more important to them than resolving the conflict. Our
approach is also simple: successfully share any difference
significant to yourself or your partner.

Peace Pilgrim (her legal name) was a vigorous senior citizen
who walked across the United States teaching her principles of
peace for this world. (If you wish more information about her, you
may write to Friends of Peace Pilgrim, 43480 Cedar Ave., Hemet,
California 92544.)

Note that all disagreements are also differences, but that not all
differences are disagreements. Unfortunately differences, significant or not, are often not recognized. If you like dogs and I like cats,

we have a difference. But if I insist that you should like cats instead of dogs, we have a disagreement.

What Do You Do With Differences?

What do you observe other people doing with differences? What do *you* do with differences? The way people relate to differences can vary considerably. Here are a few examples. When Harry doesn't get agreement or conformity with his way on emotional issues important to him, he gets frustrated up to the gills, expresses his upset with shouting and angry destruction of physical things, such as furniture, doors, walls, chairs, and material items of value to himself and others.

When Rick is confronted with an angry wife, he emotionally withdraws into silence and refuses to talk. When Flora is confronted with a demanding husband, she fights back with her own angry accusations and name-calling. All of these reactions are over differences that are not successfully shared. Mostly people do not focus on differences as such. Instead they focus on their hurt or angry feelings, blame the other for the difficulties in the situation, and frequently don't see the real differences they are dealing with. Their reaction seems to be that a difference *should not* and *must not* exist! This response makes the successful sharing of differences and disagreements difficult, if not impossible. Successful sharing is blocked by each partner's emotional demands that the other not have opposing values. When the difference you are faced with is "unacceptable" to you, do you get upset and deny the difference, or do you somehow make the difference "acceptable" to you?

Here is an easy method to recognize a difference you might have with your partner. Ask yourself these two questions:

1. What about your partner's behavior do you find annoying or objectionable?

2. What are your wants that your partner is not meeting?

Your answers will help identify your differences with your partner, but they do not identify the differences your partner may have with *you*!

If you choose to look at your partner's side, you may reverse the two questions:

1. *What about your behavior does your partner find annoying or objectionable?*

2. *What are your partner's wants that you are not meeting?*

If you choose to see the conflict between the two of you, add question #3:

3. *What are the differences between your unmet wants and your partner's unmet wants?*

These questions, when fully confronted and accepted by both you and your partner, open the door to mutual sharing; the beginning for a win-win!

Differences Over Spending Issues

Dorothy argued endlessly about money with her husband, Charles. When Al induced her to use the two sets of questions with Charles, she came up with these answers:

Dorothy's questions about herself:

Question: What about your partner's behavior do you find annoying or objectionable?

Answer: He wants to spend lavishly on food and entertainment that are soon consumed and will not last, and is miserly about spending on furniture and house renovations that will last for years.

Question: What are your wants that your partner is not meeting?

Answer: I can't get him to agree to fix up our house and get some of the furnishings, particularly a new living room set, that I really want.

Dorothy's questions about Charles's side of their arguments:

Question: What about your behavior does your partner find annoying or objectionable?

Answer: I want to spend more money fixing the house and refurnishing it, which we'll enjoy for a long time in the future, but he thinks we don't need to. And I want to cut back on eating out and on the entertainment that he thinks we can enjoy while we're still alive and kicking.

Question: What are Charles's wants that I am not meeting?

Answer: To dine out regularly at the expensive restaurants and enjoy more Broadway shows and musical concerts.

Question: What is the difference between my unmet wants and Charles's unmet wants?

Answer: We both want to spend almost equal amounts of money, but he wants to spend more of it on immediate enjoyment, while I want to spend more of it on long-terms enjoyment. He also wants to go out more to enjoy ourselves, while I want to enjoy more time at home. We agree on how much we can spend, but not what to spend most of it on.

Dorothy seemed to want long-term gratification (versus Charles wanting immediate pleasure), and she also felt that ostensibly she was more stable and disciplined in her wants than was Charles. However, when Dorothy wrote out these questions and answers, she realized that she actually wanted to enjoy her house and its furnishing on a day-to-day basis in the present and in the future. Her wants were not quite so different — or more sensible — than were Charles's.

After more clearly recognizing her differences with Charles, she challenged her beliefs that he should satisfy her wants and must not deprive her, and she gave up her anger at him. She was then able to unangrily discuss their differences, see that he was as entitled to his views as she was entitled to hers, and agreed with him on a compromise solution. Of the money left over after paying expenses and putting aside some savings, about half would be spent on dining out and entertainment, and the other half on fixing and refurnishing the house. They were not completely satisfied with that agreed-upon solution, but it worked much better than their continual arguments.

It Takes Two People to Share Successfully

Mutual sharing is often not easy to do. Why? Because we louse up our simple differences by adding complicating emotional demands that the "unacceptable" facts (such as the opposing values) should and must not exist. Thus, we translate simple differences into complicated differences. The complicated differences create most of our social problems and personal troubles.

Successfully sharing differences becomes easier when we realize the distinction between assertion and sharing. If you assert your position, but your partner misunderstands it, then sharing will not happen. Sharing happens when your partner understands your position, the way you mean it. Assertion is telling your partner what "is so" for you.

To the extent your partner understands your meaning, it is shared. It takes only one person to assert, but it takes two people to successfully share. And when your meaning is successfully shared, this is good as far as it goes. But it is only one-way sharing at that. Ultimately we are aiming for mutual, two-way sharing. Sharing a difference does not require agreement, but sharing does require receiving the message the other sends.

Unfortunately people are often unwilling to receive their partner's message and, in effect, are unwilling to share. Or, when willing to share, they don't know how to show their understanding in a way that satisfies their partner.

Dorothy, mentioned above, at first had no hesitation in telling Charles about her wanting to spend their spare money on fixing up and refurnishing their house. She was easily assertive, but she often was *angrily* assertive, and that didn't work. When she gave up her demands that Charles *absolutely should* spend their money the way she wanted to spend it, she was able to unangrily share her differences with him. Her unangry sharing encouraged Charles to in turn unangrily share his feelings with her, allowing them to arrive at an agreeable compromise regarding their spending.

When Differences Are Not Successfully Shared

Here is Ted's example of what happens when differences are not successfully shared.

My first wife and I went to a live-in school in Denmark soon after we were married. I observed how our communication usually went almost every morning. We got up at 7:00 a.m. Our conversation started on a pleasant note of sharing. Let's call this Phase 1. Soon one of us experienced being misunderstood and naturally sought to correct the misunderstanding. We'll call this Phase 2. Usually the correction was argued, and when that didn't work, we turned to explaining why the other misunderstood.

For example, I might say to her, "You are identifying me with your father. But I'm not your father. I don't use words the same way he does." Let's call this Phase 3. When the explanation failed — as it almost always did — we then resorted to name calling with the implication, "Only someone as stupid as you could possibly fail to understand such a simple point." Call this Phase 4. At this moment we seemed to have only two remaining responses to choose from: silence or violence. Fortunately, each of us chose silence. We'll call this Phase 5.

It was now 7:3O a.m. and time to go to breakfast, which we did while holding hands with a thick, hostile silence between us. Almost each morning our pattern tended to repeat in these same phases no matter the content or who felt misunderstood first.

Clearly, we had trouble with some unshared differences between us.

To my surprise I found this sequence to be more common with other people than I had originally assumed. [TC]

If you are aiming for a win-win, you may change your responses somewhat as follows:

Phase 1: *Informal sharing.* No change.

Phase 2: *Arguing the difference.* A better response than arguing is choosing *unilateral listening.* Reflect your partner's point until he confirms that you "got it."

Unfortunately, listening is often so contrary to our habits that we explain ourselves first. If explaining yourself is what you frequently do, you might find an advantage in Ben Franklin's tactic. At the end of his argument, he often added, "But of course, I might be mistaken about this matter. What do you think?" Note that he ended his argument as a non-dogmatic listening invitation.

Phase 3: *Explaining why the other misunderstood.* Instead of explaining to the other, *share* what *you* are feeling or experiencing as an "I" centered message. "I feel confused when you say, 'Yes, but....' I don't know whether you are arguing with me or supporting my point. Can you clarify for me?"

Phase 4: *Name calling.* Usually it is better to avoid put-downs entirely.

Phase 5: *Silence.* It is often better to acknowledging your partner's feelings or unmet wants. This tends to defuse unstated hostility. "Are you feeling upset because you don't experience me understanding your point?" Some people like the use of the word "feeling," so this wording works for them. But a surprising number of people object to the word "feeling" in this illustration. If this is the case, try again, leaving it out. For example, "Are you upset because you are missing my understanding of your position?"

In addition to changing your responses to your differences as suggested above, it is usually crucial that you use REBT to explore hidden "musts" that underlie and radically change your wants.

Take Al's clients Dorothy and Charles again, who fought constantly over how to spend their spare money.

I first helped Dorothy to clearly recognize her differences with Charles, and to see that they both legitimately had differences. She was able to listen more attentively to Charles, stop explaining to him why he was wrong about his wants for more dining out and more entertainment, to avoid all name-calling (which she was prone to resort to when angry), and to acknowledge his strong feelings about his unmet wants.

All of this was fine, but she still tended to slip into anger at Charles when she wanted very much to spend their money her way rather than his. I helped her see the Irrational Beliefs (IBs) that largely led to her anger:

- "Because I am so nice to Charles in general, he shouldn't prevent me from getting the furnishings I want."
- "Because I would enjoy refurnishing our living room greatly, he should be eager to have us refurnish it."
- "Because fixing the house and refurnishing it would give us years of satisfaction, I should be able to do this."
- "Charles can't even see the virtue of my wants and therefore has no respect for me, as he must."

I showed Dorothy that her *desires* were quite sensible and legitimate, but that her raising them to *demands* was unrealistic, illogical, and rage-provoking, which encouraged Charles to fight against them and to deny them. When she saw this, she realistically understood that there was no reason why Charles absolutely should agree to her wants — especially when he had opposing wants of his own. It was illogical to think that because she greatly wanted a refurnished home, that he had to go along with her desires. If she insisted on these unrealistic and illogical demands, she would only make herself enraged, and make Charles less likely to give in to them. [AE]

When Dorothy saw the irrationality of her demands and unilaterally changed them to preferences, Charles was able to see and give up his own demandingness. Then they agreed to disagree and to work out some win-win compromises.

Differences Are Not Always Obvious

Why is it so difficult for people to see their differences with
each other?

When I first starting looking at differences, I mistakenly thought
that any difference was obvious to people, and felt extremely
puzzled when others asked, "What is a difference?" I thought,
"Can't they see a difference when it is in front of them?"

Unfortunately, the answer is, "No, they often don't see a
difference when it is in front of them." What they may see is how
right they are and how wrong the other is, or how unfair the other
is, or how the other is upsetting them, without conscious awareness
of a difference.

I decided to confront the question, "What is a difference?" and
discovered that a difference is *any* contrast! Innocent contrasts are
sometimes important. For example, I was in a gift shop at the Dallas
airport that had a glass wall and a glass door. Hearing a loud crash,
I turned to see that a lady had tried to walk through the glass wall,
thinking it was the open glass door. She had not clearly
distinguished the contrast between the door opening and the wall.
Indeed, the contrast was hard to see, but still possible if one looked
closely enough. [TC]

A small difference may be a significant difference. Good
communication includes noticing "innocent" contrasts between
what people say and what they do, and especially noticing
contrasts between what they believe and what you believe. While
allowing for the existence of a difference, also be willing to explore
your partner's side.

If you intend to move toward a win-win by means of sharing
significant differences in beliefs or values, our Fourth Guideline
may be for you. Here again is how we word the *Fourth Guideline:*
Share and explore differences with your partner to move toward a
better resolution that accepts parts of both your views. Or agree to
disagree.

Additionally, be ready to compromise without pretending
that you agree when you really don't agree.

The Revolving Discussion Sequence (RDS): A Way to Cooperative Dialogue

Now that we have some clarity about what a difference is, we will look at one way to successfully share differences and disagreements: Revolving Discussion Sequence (RDS). With your good intentions, this process can actually serve to move you and your partner toward a better resolution. It also accepts parts of both your partner's views and yours. "Move toward" is a key phrase here. There is no guarantee that you will immediately get a win-win, but you can still move in that direction, and eventually get there.

In the 1960s Ted had a Revolving Discussion Sequence (RDS) Growth Group which served as a communication laboratory. Of the many people who went through this group, Lynn stands out in memory more than all others. When Lynn joined this group, she had just been kicked out of her home by her husband. At the same time, inconsistently, he gave her a new car for her birthday. The two of them had fights over sex, how to raise their four children, and how to manage their money. His response was to insist that she leave. She rented a small apartment, earned money giving piano lessons, and dated other men.

The group never directly related to any of these issues in Lynn's life. Instead the group helped Lynn to absorb the process and the principles of formal RDS, Revolving Discussion Sequence, which she then flexibly applied to her family situation. Two of the children sided with her and the other two sided with her husband. She invented new ways of using formal RDS, along with new applications of informal RDS. Eventually she succeeded in reuniting her family. Read what Lynn wrote in 1973 about RDS.

⌒ ⌒ ⌒

I first heard the word "cooperate" from my third grade teacher, Miss Pinner. She introduced the word with her usual intense seriousness, and total lack of humor. "Good boys and girls always cooperate," she said to the class, "at school, at home, and in public."

I went home, tasting the word between my lips. "I'm going to cooperate everywhere," I told my mother as I put down my lunch pail.

"Fine," she said, giving the bread an extra punch. "If you just manage to cooperate at home, I'll be grateful."

I questioned my grandfather who knew all. Hadn't he taught me the alphabet by my second birthday, and been the source of other great wisdom? He leafed through the dictionary in its place of honor on his desk. "Cooperate, hmm," he smiled, his gold teeth gleaming in the light. "Yes, it means to get along."

I pondered the idea. Getting along with everyone seemed overwhelming now that I thought about it. I could hear my mother's voice saying crossly, "I wish for once you and your sister would get along." So I tucked the word away, and went about the business of growing up.

Recently I went to the dictionary again and looked the word up for myself. "Cooperate," I read. "Working together for mutual benefit." Of course, I thought, doesn't everyone know the importance of working together and helping each other? But I felt unsatisfied. The definition of just getting along somehow didn't seem enough, at least not in the field of communication, which I've been exploring and teaching for the last decade.

The answer, of course, is "yes." Most people are well aware of the importance of working together and the importance of talking together in a mutually helpful way. The trouble is, hardly any of us have been taught how to do this effectively.

When I first introduced communication classes at the American Institute of Family Relations in Redondo Beach, California, five years ago, I asked the beginning students what seemed to be their main difficulty. Nine out of ten replied, "I just don't seem to be able to communicate," or "My wife (husband, sister, mother, child) just won't communicate with me."

Generally speaking, they knew their communications were fouled up, but in trying to narrow down the problem, they didn't quite know what was wrong. Learning to communicate well is not some mysterious gift from outer space. It is a skill that can be learned just as we learn to swim, play the piano, or dance. And that skill, in order to be most effective, needs to include an active, participatory sharing; in short, mutual cooperation.

To teach clients the simple basics of good cooperative dialogue, I use a technique called Revolving Discussion Sequence (RDS). The formal structure, developed by Ted Crawford, teacher, and Luis Ijams, accountant, consists of three steps:

- UNDERSTANDING
- AGREEMENT
- STATEMENT

These steps are based on the not-so-unique, but seldom-followed idea, that good communication includes really listening to each other, giving the other person support for his or her point of view, being open to change and growth, and leveling about what we think and feel. It also involves taking turns, rather than both talking at once.

In RDS classes and workshops, I am consistently delighted during our lesson on UNDERSTANDING at the expressions of amazement that occur when a client realizes his or her spouse is actually *trying* to hear what he or she is saying, instead of cooking up a rebuttal in his or her head. Half the battle is won when in the heat of an argument one of the partners can say, and mean it, "Okay, I'll listen to you first.

Although simple in structure, RDS asks for a commitment from those who use it, a commitment to the idea that communication is a valuable commodity in today's world, and worthwhile pursuing actively. It operates on the premise that in order to be free emotionally, we will commit ourselves to be willing to talk about anything, and that if the other desires to talk first, we will do our best to understand what he or she is saying.

This is not as easy as it might seem. Here is an example from a recent RDS workshop. Marcia and John, a young couple married two years, have been considering separation. Their reason? "We don't communicate," says John with a sour look. Our reason? They are parallel monologuists — Ted Crawford's term for people who will talk like two trains running down parallel tracks. They never connect.

We asked John and Marcia to show us a specific. That was easy. They chose a fight they'd had that morning. This is what had happened.

Marcia (angrily): "Someone walked off with my handbag today. And I had fifty dollars in cash in it along with all my credit cards."

John (replying with sarcasm): "I keep telling you to watch what you're doing."

With this lead-off, the ensuing battle continued to rage for three hours before they had to leave for class. And from the rather pointed looks they had been exchanging during the class lecture-demonstration hour, it was still raging non-verbally. I asked if they'd be willing to be guinea pigs. They agreed to air their grievances.

I asked Marcia to start, as she seemed most triggered, and I gave John instruction that he was to listen carefully and put into his own words what Marcia said, checking back with her to see if he was on target.

Marcia (warily): "Well, it's like I said. Someone walked off with my handbag today, and I had fifty dollars in cash in it (tears came to her eyes) and all my credit cards!"

John: "Yeah, and it's like I said before...."

"Wait a minute," I jumped in. "Remember, John, the first step is UNDERSTANDING. You'll have your turn to talk later. What did you hear Marcia say?"

John: "Uh, oh, yes. Marcia, you said someone just walked off with your purse, and your credit cards were in it. And fifty dollars cash."

"Now, check with her," I reminded him.

John: "Yeah, is that what you said?"

Marcia (tearfully): "Yes.

"Good," I said. "Now to complete the UNDERSTANDING you might reflect back what she seems to be feeling."

John: "You seem pretty upset about it. Is that right?"

Marcia: "You know it!" (A look of relief settled on her face.)

"Now try the second step," I told him. "Give her some AGREEMENT."

John: "I can see that you do feel badly about it. I would too if someone swiped my billfold. In fact, I remember once someone stole my skates when I was a kid. I still feel a little sore when I think about it."

Marcia (now laughing and crying at the same time) bursts in: "Wow, it feels so good to have you on my side, to feel you really care about what happened, instead of blaming me."

"All right, John," I said, "Now the sequence revolves, and while you make your STATEMENT, which is the third step, Marcia will try to UNDERSTAND your point of view."

John (thoughtfully): "I know you can't help it when someone steals something from you, but I also know you've been concerned about misplacing or forgetting things recently."

Marcia: "Oh, you mean about me leaving my tennis racquet in the restaurant, and misplacing the income tax material?"

John: "That's right. So maybe you've had a lot on your mind, and we could put our heads together later, and see if there's any way I can help!"

"Bravo," I applauded.

Marcia (still in the UNDERSTANDING step): "Are you saying two heads are better than one, and you want to be friends?"

John (grinning): "Something like that."

Marcia: "Well, I'll agree to that. I like your offer to help because I have been losing things lately. Sometimes I think I need two heads."

This brings laughter from the class, and Marcia and John go back to their seats holding hands.

In the Revolving Discussion Dialogue, (RDS), John doesn't attack. He listens first, then supports Marcia's position, before speaking his own piece. When she finds him open, and offering help instead of blame, she can look at what needs correcting instead of becoming defensive, and their relationship grows instead of deteriorates. This is the essence of cooperation.

Can you learn cooperative dialogue on your own?

"Yes!" says Ted, emphatically. Below is some homework suggested by him.

〜 〜 〜

- To practice **UNDERSTANDING**:

Tell the other person in your own words what you think you have heard her say. Then check it out with her: "Is that what you meant?" "Am I with your meaning?" "Am I hearing you right?" Or use a similar confirmation.

When she says "yes" (and she is the judge of whether or not she has been understood), move on to give some agreement.

- To practice *AGREEMENT*:

Find something in what he said, felt, or meant to agree with: "I agree that..." "That's an intriguing point of view..." "I like what you said about...." However you word it, there is always something you can agree with or affirm that shows him that you positively value him.

- To practice *STATEMENT-making*:

Share yourself by verbalizing what is happening inside of you: "I think..." "I feel..." "I see..." "I like..." "I don't like..." "I wonder..." "I see the situation differently..."

These "I" sentences can help you reach out to the other person instead of creating barriers with words that attack or distort. When you have practiced these three stages with your partner (at least thirty minutes a day is recommended), I think you will begin to notice some exciting changes.

What if the other person doesn't know these rules? Can RDS work anyway?

Again, a qualified "yes." Genuine caring and interest shown by your willingness to really listen, by finding something to agree with before you share your disagreement, and by directly counting yourself in, encourages the same in return. It may not seem so immediately, but subtly and surely the relationship changes and deepens.

My own first experience with RDS was a shock. I attended an RDS workshop given by Ted in 1963. I prided myself on my ability to listen well because my teachers in grade school used to comment on my being a "good listener." What they didn't realize was that I had made a fine point of gazing at them with a rapt expression, letting their words flow in one ear and out the other, while my brain wandered off to create fantastic stories that would have put Superwoman to shame. In checking out what I thought I heard people say at the workshop, and later at home, I discovered I automatically tuned out most of what my husband said to me. I was still using my rapt expression, while my brain went its own way. I made a decision. Superwoman would have to go. Fantasies are fun, but not when they lead to turning off the emotional hearing aid.

So I practiced my new-found techniques, and as usual with anything new, I goofed. I tried too hard. I sounded awkward and stilted. But came the time, and not too long after I started, when I became aware of a new quality in our exchanges, a tenderness and trust that led me to experience "cooperation" in a way that far exceeds the idea of merely getting along. Working together began to take on a different meaning for me.

The discipline and practice to develop new communication patterns has had many payoffs for me. It can for you, too. Mine, are the deepening of my relationship with my husband and friends, and an exciting kind of family sharing. There is the growing knowledge that we can talk freely about anything, and a trusting that each member really cares about hearing what the other has to say. RDS was, for us, a tool we first learned as a way to help change our outmoded communication patterns and, later, to create our own approaches to fit our individual family unit.

Cooperative dialogue can be the kind of experience one has of warmth, camaraderie, as well as working together for mutual benefit. A taking of turns, and thinking about what's best for US, a delicious human happening. [Lynn]

∿ ∿ ∿

Note that Lynn suggests flexibility, adapting RDS — a non-adversarial form of communication — to fit your situation, after you have learned to work the three steps.

Suggestions for Using RDS in Informal Communication

There are basically two communication roles: the Sender Role and the Receiver Role. Both are equally important. From an RDS perspective, you are responsible for the message you send. And you are responsible for the message you receive. Each person in each role is responsible for the messages exchanged between them. The informal application of Revolving Discussion Sequence (RDS) calls for you being flexible as you combine the two roles of sender and receiver in the ever-changing world of ordinary dialogue.

The Receiver Role:

• *Ask questions to clarify your partner's meaning.* The most frequent condition of human communication is that *the message received is not the message sent*! A wife saw a note her husband wrote that said "Feelings out!" she interpreted that to mean that he intended to rule out expressing his feelings when communicating.

When she asked him about it, he told her it was a reminder to himself to express himself — to get his feelings out. Just the opposite of her assumption! For various reasons, communication is frequently very ambiguous. Ask questions, empathetically or sympathetically, to clarify your partner's meaning. Be sure to distinguish between clarifying questions and challenging questions. Challenging and rhetorical questions belong in the Sender Role, not the Receiver Role. When you use challenging questions, you already know your answer to your own question. With clarifying questions, you are seeking to understand what you are unclear about.

• *Often your partner may not know how to say what he or she means.* Therefore, when your partner feels confused, you may not want to confront your partner. Now is the time to help him or her to express the deeper meaning. Understanding another is a moving target. In mirroring your partner's meaning, you adopt a flexible attitude and change your view as your partner changes his or her meaning. Then there are two people working at getting one person clear. Your partner is not so alone in being confused.

• *Connect before you correct.* By "connect" we mean to empathize with your partner's feelings, goals, unmet wants, or issues before you seek to correct or help him or her. If you are like most people you immediately jump in to help your partner solve his or her problem, thus you mistakenly put *problem-solving* before *connecting* — perhaps thinking that solving the other's problem is the same as connecting? *Problem→Solution* is the sequence used. This sequence often invites a "Yes, but..." type of response. Before you try to solve your partner's problem, open yourself up and listen with your heart — which is what we mean by "connecting." That is, see and hear your partner's problem from his or her perspective.

Jane could see that Jack, her husband, had a problem with money and that she had the solution to his problem. First, he denied that he had a problem. Her solution was to persuade him to acknowledge that he had it as defined by her. Then she would persuade him to give his credit cards to her so that he couldn't use them. And lastly, to let her manage all of the money. She went ahead with this plan and it mostly worked. Her *Problem→Solution* approach solved the practical problem. However, the emotional problems, both his and hers, still remained unresolved. As Ted talked with her, she revealed that she still felt deeply hurt, not because of the huge debt Jack had built up, but because by denying his problem, he betrayed her trust in him. Jack denied there was a practical problem, and didn't talk the situation over with her, as she thought he *should* have done, of course. "That," she reported, "is what hurts!" She never empathetically explored his side of the issue.

Conveniently for Jane, *Jack* has the problem and *she* has the solution. This way of viewing often makes her seem right and makes him seem wrong. Being noble and generous, she immediately seeks to correct her partner with her solutions, but usually leaves out his feelings. Unfortunately, this is a one-way communication street.

A better sequence could have been: *Problem→Understanding→Solution*. Here "understanding" means understanding Jack's side, his way. We can guess that Jack felt resentment and humiliation. By exploring these feelings, both his practical problem and his emotional problems could be understood and related to.

If Jane had tried connecting before correcting, she could empathetically ask, "Jack, are you feeling resentment because you are wanting and not getting respect from me?" At first, this way of communication may seem risky — until she got used to it.

Alternatively, of course, Jack might risk connecting with his wife's upsetness when she attacked him, by trying something like, "Jane, are you deeply troubled because you are missing our collaborating together on money matters?" He would then be connecting with her feelings before explaining his side.

• *All listening is selective.* You listen for something, usually something important to *yourself*, such as support for your self-appraisal, approval, what interests you, agreement with what you said, how responsive your partner is to you, a question you want answered, etc. All these considerations are significant. But, for the moment, put them all on the back burner. Instead, *listen for what is important to your partner*, such as his feelings, unmet wants, emphasis, explanation, position, or significant issues.

• *Treat illogical statements as an "and/also" instead of an "either/or."* If your mate paradoxically says that "up is down," and this does not make logical sense to you, you may ask a question of clarification. Or, you may mirror it back as an "and/also." "In your world, an object is both up *and also* down at the same time," and then wait for clarification from your partner. Don't say anything like, "That makes absolutely no sense to me. Something can't be both up and down at the same time. It has to be either one way or the other way. It is either black or white."

The Receiver Role

In Formal RDS, the Receiver uses both the RDS Understanding Step and the RDS Agreement Step. See what you honestly appreciate or agree with about your partner's position and share your agreement. "That's true." "Yes." "Wonderful!" "I like…." "That's a good idea." "I agree." "What you said is important because…." "I like your attitude." "You remind me of myself when you said…." "Your wording expresses my feeling so well." "The implications of your idea (suggestion, opinion, position) are significant."

The RDS Agreement Step is a powerful way to connect with your partner. When that doesn't work, as occasionally it won't, reflect your understanding of your partner's intention or meaning as in the Understanding Step. "That was an expensive restaurant," you say, intending to show some agreement. And your partner says something like, "The expense is not my point. What I'm getting at is your mother didn't like my taking her out for lunch." At such a point, you drop your agreement and understandingly mirror back something like, "You feel disappointed with my mother's lack of appreciation when you seek to include her. Is that your meaning?"

The Sender Role:

- When using informal RDS, break up your position into a series of brief statements. Don't overload your listener with a lot of information all at once.

- Usually include your feelings when stating your position.

- First, preface your difference or disagreement with something you honestly do support or agree with. State your position as something for your partner to consider rather than as something that must be agreed with. Gently seek to make a "safe space" for your mate to express his or her difference or disagreement to your viewpoint. Make a point of appreciating the fact of your partner's disagreement with you. Welcome such differences as enriching the communication between you.

• Remember that every position is worth considering, especially your partner's position. Respond to his or her position or behavior with respect.

• Assert your own position with respect, rather than apologetically.

• Think of differences as natural, something to share and explore, rather than as sabotaging of your position.

• Usually avoid *shoulds* and *musts*. Use "It would be better if..." or, "We preferably should do this."

Emotional Disturbance

Emotional disturbance is the biggest barrier, but not the only difficulty, to the successful sharing of differences and disagreements and creating a win-win position. Here is the REBT succinct overview of emotional disturbance.

Practically all emotional disturbance arises from

• *blaming oneself* — which leads to feelings of anxiety, guilt, depression, lack of confidence, and self-depreciation;

• *blaming others* — which leads to feelings of anger, hostility, childish rebellion, grandiosity, and social conflict; and

• *blaming fate or the universe* — which leads to feelings of self-pity, and the compulsion to control everyone and everything in an arbitrary, dictatorial manner.

Note that blaming follows from your objection to factual "reality." This objection often leads you to have conflicts with others. Mostly, you feel as you think. However, your thoughts, feelings and behavior go together and influence each other. You might also note that blaming is a negative judgmental thought about the "reality," but is not the "reality" itself.

Sharing Differences Successfully

We have suggested using Revolving Discussion Sequence as one way to successfully share differences and disagreements and arrive at a win-win solution. And when emotionality gets in your way, we suggested using REBT. Indeed, Rational Emotive Behavior Therapy is the foundation for RDS, and can be the foundation for almost any approach for successfully sharing differences, disagreements, and moving toward a win-win solution, if you choose to use it for this purpose.

We find that individual couples tend to evolve their own unique style for what they do with differences and disagreements. For Lynn and her husband that style included both formal and informal RDS. How you learn to share differences successfully in your relationships is your communication challenge. The sharing of differences and disagreements is a moving target in a growing relationship. Sometimes you will be successful and sometimes not. Focus on *improvement*, not on *perfection*. It would be good to set aside a regular time for a "gripe session," when both you and your partner can practice formal RDS and openly share your complaints and wishes about each other and your relationship.

Formal RDS includes conflict, but also goes beyond it. In a very real way RDS expresses the view of Virginia Satir, "We come together on our similarities and grow on our differences." When disagreements are successfully shared, differences become smaller and fewer and similarities increase — contrary to many people's expectations.

The key to Guideline 4 is the intention and attitude "to move toward a better resolution." The successful sharing of differences does not mean you try to share all disagreements. There are too many differences for this to be practical. *Your intention here is to willingly talk and share about anything significant to your partner or yourself.* Each person defines "significant" in her or his own way. Successful sharing often produces agreement, but does not necessarily require agreement.

That genius, Anonymous, once said, "One of the secrets of life is to make stepping stones out of stumbling blocks." There likely will be some stumbling blocks that get in your way before you and your partner have created your own workable style for successful sharing. Persist, explore, experiment. Virginia Satir expressed a central REBT value when she said, "Life is not the way it's *supposed* to be. It's the way *it is.* The way you cope with it is what makes the difference." REBT and RDS provide two ways to cope with your communication stumbling blocks. Satir added another good REBT value: "I think if I have one message, the one thing before I die that most of the world would know, *it would be that the event does not determine how to respond to the event.* That is a purely personal matter. The way in which we respond will direct and influence the event more than the event itself."

Our intention is to enable you to listen to anything without unduly upsetting yourself. Your difficulty in successfully sharing differences and disagreements comes from getting emotionally upset over listening to what you don't want to hear. The biggest communication problem of many people is their unconscious Double Bind commandment: *Be honest with me, but don't tell me what I don't want to hear.* With REBT and RDS, you can learn to remove your part of communicating poorly with your partner.

In the next chapter, we look at one way you can lovingly support your relationship with your partner.

9

Guideline 5:
Support Your Partner's Goals

Support your partner's goals and purposes. Don't surrender your own integrity and your own important desires and views, but go as far as you honestly can to support your partner even when you clearly disagree.

The fifth guideline emphasizes loving in a giving, active way. A psychologist friend, Jewel, told us she not only supported it enthusiastically, but that she had largely figured it out herself. She always went out of her way to support her fiancé's purposes, goals, wishes, and wants, even when they were opposed to her own. For example, he was a very conservative, profit-oriented business owner whose main concern was the pursuit of money, while she was a socially interested do-gooder who worked ceaselessly, at modest remuneration, to help her low-income clinic population, and really enjoyed giving much extra time and energy to benefit them. She not only never criticized her fiancé's purposes and (almost unethical) actions, but supported him lovingly and praised his (often dubious) accomplishments, giving him real love, but secretly holding on to her own important desires and ethics. Al had a talk with Jewel and noted:

She made it sound great, and I almost thoroughly bought it at first. However, in observing Jewel and her fiancé, I noticed that she subserviently went along with his every whim because, as far as I could see, she absolutely needed his total approval and was anxious and lost by its absence. When with him, she was what I call a "love slob," and had no will of her own.

Noting this, I suspected and was able to find some evidence for Jewel's unusual devotion to her low-income clients. As in the case of her fiancé, she direly needed their approval, and sacrificed considerable time and effort to get it, thus "proving" how worthwhile she was. [AE]

So, instead of giving love unconditionally, as she honestly thought she did, Jewel gave it very conditionally. She got the "good" results she wanted or needed, but she wasn't really "herself" and therefore lacked integrity. This is not what we mean by Guideline 5.

Marshall Rosenberg, director of the Center for Compassionate Communication in Sherman, Texas, tells the story of a wife who asked her husband to give up spending so much time playing cards with "the boys." He decided to please her and started playing golf instead. The wife was furious because she expected that he would spend more time with her and that expectation was not met. She told him what she *didn't* want, but did not say what she *did* want! Communication 101 may be to state what you want without expecting your partner to be a mind reader.

Suppose the husband had asked his wife, "What do you expect would happen if I gave up playing cards with the boys?" She might answer, "You would spend more time with me." He then would have a clearer idea of what she really wanted. You might discover what your partner *really* wants by asking your partner, "What would you expect to happen if I stopped doing what you don't want?" This question only *sometimes* gets you a clear answer of what your partner wants.

Ted decides to skip the mind-reading:

My wife, Jolanta, occasionally expects me to read her mind, and gets upset when I can't. When I observe that she may be a little upset, I now usually guess and inquire about what she might feel and what her unmet want might be. "Are you thinking that I should be sensitive to how tired you feel, and are you wanting me to fix dinner?" Over time, I'm improving in my guesses. Such guessing and inquiring is excellent practice for me.

Here is another scenario: When Jolanta is *angry* with me (not just a little upset), I usually also feel angry at her and focus on my own shoulds, hurt, and anger. I may remind her, with a sharp edge in my voice, that I also have a side worth considering. My resentment, hurt, or anger always has a "should" or two embedded in it somewhere. First, I notice how justified I think I am. Second, I think Jolanta should see what is so obviously right about my position. But then I also believe that *everyone* has something right about his or her position, no matter how crazy *I* think it might be. And, if this is true, then Jolanta has something right about her position. What might that something right be?

Usually, but not always, I later unilaterally explore Jolanta's side in some depth without explaining or defending my position. When she is upset with me, I often make a point to reach out to her in one way or another after I've handled my own upsetness. I might say, "Jolanta, I want to understand you, your way. Were you feeling anger at me when you slammed the door?" (Or whatever she said or did that serves as my cue that all is not right with her.) Whatever she says I mirror back to her, "Let's see if I understand you correctly. Are you meaning...?" (And here I may do more guessing.) "Is that what you are getting at?" When she confirms that I do, indeed, understand her, her way, I may ask, "Is there anything more that you want to share with me?"

When I explore Jolanta's feelings in depth, I'm hoping to answer two questions:

- What does she want?
- What is her basic attitude?

The answer to these two questions usually emerges as we explore her justifications for her position. For example, what she may want is that I assume some responsibility for doing the household tasks. Along with and underneath her want usually is her attitude of what she thinks is fair. Jolanta, like many of us, is sometimes unclear about what her purposes, goals, wishes, or wants are. If I choose to use Guideline 5, and I do, I take it as my responsibility to gently assist Jolanta in discovering what her wants might be. After that is done, I then explore inside myself what I can honestly do to support her wants without surrendering my own integrity. [TC]

The late psychologist Carl Rogers once stated that only very small children and very mature adults clearly know what they want. The vast majority of people, he implied (though we doubt Dr. Rogers would say it this way), are too neurotic to know what they really want when they have emotional problems. Assuming he may be right about this matter, we give the REBT explanation by observing that the vast majority of people often confuse what they *really* want with what they think they *should* want. Very few individuals have a clear life purpose, a list of specific goals, or intelligent decisions about their own wishes and wants. When we clear away their dogmatic *shoulds* about doing "this" and *musts* about doing "that," their underlying purposes, goals, wishes, and wants emerge more clearly.

Along with Guideline 5 we emphasize the giving of support in a loving way. Therefore, it is useful to understand love in a giving way. Not all people, unfortunately, understand love as giving.

In my original version of *How to Live with a Neurotic*, I wrote that when a disturbed person says, "I love you," he or she really means, "How wonderful to have you love me and thereby make me worthwhile." "Neurotics," I said, "often fall violently in love: that is, they become obsessed with individuals they would like to love them. But they have little ability to give love; to want to help a person achieve his or her own growth and happiness for their own ends." [AE]

This kind of focus is on getting — not giving — love, and it leads to much miscommunication. To maturely communicate with your partner, use Guideline 5 to focus on a truly giving kind of love.

Loving and Giving

To support giving love is a creative challenge which Ted and Jolanta experience in a special way. Jolanta is a Catholic and, as an agnostic, Ted is not even a Christian.

When I asked Jolanta what her life purpose was, she answered, "To experience more of the love of God." I'm not sure there is a God, let alone that He has love to give, so I wondered, "How can I support Jolanta's purpose when it is so vague? How might I do so without violating my own self-respect or integrity?" Initially, this was a creative challenge for me. Indeed, it still is. I explored possibilities in my mind, and eventually developed a workable approach.

I observed that her channel for experiencing the love of God was to attend mass. Okay, then I would attend mass with her, just to be supportive. I don't have to do anything special, other than just be with her emotionally. I am not there to change her, to persuade her to another point of view, or to agree or disagree with her. This in itself is a challenge to me. But, when I went to mass with Jolanta, I often found myself bored, and getting bored was not supportive of her.

By meeting the challenge of boredom, I changed my experience of attending mass and changed our relationship for the better. I decided to allow myself to feel bored while I also experienced "elements of newness" that occurred for me during mass. The "elements of newness" provided interest and freshness to the usual ritual of mass, significantly reducing or sometimes totally eliminating the boredom. I shared those "elements of newness" with her after mass. After a short time she also noticed "elements of newness" for herself and shared those with me as well. Now, after almost every mass, we get a bite to eat and together share our "elements of newness.

Frequently, mass serves as a place of meditation where something said or done during mass inspires some insight into a problem I am struggling with. I almost never prejudge how good or valuable an "element of newness" might be. My "elements of newness" might be pure trivia, highly significant to me, or somewhere in between. Most are incidental or trivial, but all are fun to share.

As an example of trivia, in church I might notice how many light bulbs are burned out, or how many windows are open on a hot day; I focus on the flower arrangement, or on how I like or dislike the singing of the choir.

As a more profound example of an "element of newness," I once observed my emotional reaction to a statue of the Virgin Mary when the summer light coming through a window made the statue appear very beautiful. I admired the skill of the sculptor, and how he had made the statue seem alive. It was obviously a piece of art created with much love. To my surprise, and contrary to my agnostic beliefs, I "fell in love" with the Virgin Mary as if she were a real live woman. Suddenly, I realized how it could be that Catholics could emotionally believe inconsistent things, and see them as a mystery to be accepted, without logically disturbing their faith.

An "element of newness" comes when you experience something as if you see it for the "first time" with a sense of freshness. You, of course, have seen a sunset before, but a particular sunset may seem "new." I have experienced Jolanta as beautiful before, but today her beauty is renewed, alive again, and fresh. I almost always experience an "element of newness" during mass. Everyone experiences "elements of newness" in certain life situations, but they are often discounted or slip by unnoticed.

The point of all this is that offering loving support for your partner's purposes, goals, wishes, and wants can be a rewarding and stimulating challenge. You can make it an ongoing project available to you without requiring that you get love at the same time.

Jolanta and I almost never concern ourselves with how trivial or profound, or how positive or negative an "element of newness" might be. Anything can be grist for our mill. Our sharing of "elements of newness" may lead into exploring our relationship, poetry, family values, our past history, Christianity, Buddhism, Hinduism, Islam, theology, psychology, gossip, investing our money, politics, economics, history, or almost any subject you might think of. Sometimes our "elements of newness" give us good mileage. Or, we may not go anywhere with a specific "element of newness" beyond just mentioning it and sharing it. We do not require any specific results from sharing our "elements of newness"; they are a pleasure in and of themselves. [TC]

Integrity

Our perception of integrity is a little different from the dictionary definition, and we think it is worth your consideration. We define integrity as "honestly accepting beliefs or evidence that conflict with your own view of the "facts" and changing your position accordingly." When you have integrity, you confront and wrestle with your own inconsistencies, dilemmas, and fears, so that you are free to grow and evolve toward your own self-actualization. Integrity is a function of "truth" as you thoughtfully understand it, at the moment, while you keep the flexibility to change your understanding as you confront disconfirming data or beliefs.

Al has had a bit of trouble with many clients who have great traditional integrity in that they honestly uphold their own unpopular views, even when others penalize them for having such views.

However, I sometimes advise them to keep their opinions to themselves, and more efficiently get on with their business and personal relationships.

Mack thought most sporting events were "childish" and "idiotic," and volubly said so at his office. He greatly antagonized several of his coworkers, causing them to sabotage some of his scheduling work, and almost getting him fired. While he still hated sporting events, by keeping his mouth shut when a big game approached, he got along much better with his coworkers.

Mack held his honest opinions about sports rigidly and dogmatically; he could see nothing good about sports. So he had integrity — traditional integrity — plus closed mindedness. I had a hard time getting him to acknowledge the benefits of any sports or sporting events, but he had an easy time ranting about the disadvantages. As an REBT homework assignment, he was given the "sport" of finding something good about sports. He came up with the idea that sports gave many people great enjoyment, and directly and indirectly led to considerable employment. With this better view, he was able to still dislike sports, but not rigidly and intemperately. [AE]

In intimate relations, integrity is still honest and usually fine. But again, it often doesn't work if it is one-sided. Another of Al's clients, Vera, hated smokers.

They were, according to her, not only killing themselves but other people as well, by polluting the atmosphere. Hal, her husband, largely saw her point and had stopped his occasional smoking completely when he started to date her. That was fine, but she still acted obnoxiously by crusading obsessively and compulsively against public smokers, bullying friends even if they privately smoked, talking endlessly against smoking, and almost getting into fistfights with people who smoked in permitted areas of restaurants. Enough was enough! Hal insisted that Vera get help with her annoying obsession.

I showed Vera, in REBT sessions, that Hal admired her courageous integrity. After all, she was willing to stick to her ground and lose some of their best friends (some gave up smoking in her presence, but still "nauseatingly reeked of smoke"). But Hal also pointed out that he had had his fill, was thoroughly sick of her obsessive-compulsive behavior, thought she was going too far, and definitely didn't want to be restricted by her turning off so many people. Even though he agreed with her antismoking stand, he disagreed with her manner of promulgating it and, while not hating *Vera*, Hal was hating some of her *ways*.

With my help, Vera began to keep her disgust of smoking to herself, and immediately got along much better with Hal and their friends. Good! But she still felt enraged at smokers and kept silently churning her own gut about their "terrorism" against non-smokers. So I suggested that she use the REBT exercise of referenting the cost-benefit ratio of smoking. She made a list of many items that reminded her of the non-intentional foolishness of smokers and the harm they were doing. Her list included these "good" reasons for smoking:

• Smokers often don't realize the harm they are doing to others; they are truly ignorant.

• Smokers repress the harm they are doing to themselves, or they are really too stupid to see it.

• When smokers realize how bad smoking is, they are often seriously addicted to it. They can only stop with enormous difficulty.

• Some smokers use smoking as a pacifier. They are very anxious and it temporarily helps them to allay their anxiety.

• Some smokers have nothing better to do to ward off boredom.

• Some smokers are in physical pain and only get relief from smoking.

• Some smokers work better while smoking, such as a writer working on a difficult piece.

• There are people who enjoy smoking and practically nothing else in life.

• Some people smoke to help their addicted mates who can't stop, and who would feel very guilty if they smoked alone.

• Some teenagers smoke because their friends do, and they would be ridiculed if they didn't do so, too.

Vera wrote down her list of "good" or "excusable" reasons why some people smoke and went over it in her head several times each day. After doing so for a month, she became much more tolerant of many smokers. She still opposed smoking, contributed to anti-smoking educational causes, and risked offending some people with her strong views. But she flexibly acknowledged the fact that smoking might not be totally bad for everyone all of the time, and became more accepting of smokers. Hal appreciated her working at toleration and considered her doing so a gift of love to him. Their communication and intimacy with each other greatly improved. [AE]

When you relate supportively to your partner's purpose, goal, wish, or want, it is important to allow your partner the right to be wrong and to make mistakes. We look further at this challenging issue in the next chapter.

10

Guideline 6:
Give Your Partner
The Right To Be Wrong

Give your partner the right to be wrong. Respect both of your rights to be fallible humans — your inalienable right to make mistakes and to learn from your own experiences and errors. Don't honor only your right to be an error-prone person!

A l originated the phrase, "the right to be wrong," when he first started to use REBT.
I saw that most human disturbance follows almost immediately after people see human mistakes yet refuse to grant themselves and others the privilege of making mistakes. I have, since that time, helped countless individuals, in my therapy sessions, my talks and workshops, and my writings and cassettes, to be less disturbed. Including myself! [AE]

Indeed, "the right to be wrong" is almost axiomatic. Humans are human, and therefore exceptionally fallible. They are born that way and they are reared to be that way. No escaping! Obviously, then, they have the privilege, the prerogative, and the right to make countless errors and mistakes during their lifetimes. How could they not do so?

What's more, though you as a fallible human learn many things by trial and error, you have the right — again, the privilege — to fail to learn by your mistakes, to make the same stupid errors again and again. Definitely. Indubitably. Go, if you will, make the same blunders again and again, though you suffered from them last time. By all means recognize your failings and, we hope, learn to fail less in the future. But you don't *have* to learn. Nor to blame yourself for not learning. You still have the right, almost a sacred right, to be wrong.

Flora was a perfectionist who blamed the man she lived with, Denny, for almost every mistake he made, in business, in the relationship, with his friends, in sports ... you name it. Denny gave Flora the right to be wrong and to be "unfairly" critical of him. But she berated him in front of others, especially his business associates, who might therefore think him less capable than he was. He tried to get her to do it only when they were alone together, when he could use REBT principles to allow himself to dislike it but not to upset himself about it. To no avail. She kept putting his "defeats" out in public — to "help" him, of course — and actually helped to ruin his associates' confidence in him. Denny threatened to "trade her in" for a non-perfectionistic partner, and after a while he meant it.

Flora saw that Denny was determined to stop her public criticism, but was not emotionally upset about it because of his REBT training. So she arranged for several REBT sessions with Al. She learned that even though some of her criticisms of Denny were factually correct — for example, he used bad grammar and refused to correct it — he had the right to be "wrong" and didn't have to be right. Her constant public carping, moreover, was particularly "wrong" for several reasons:

1. It harmed Denny in his business relationships.

2. It made her less lovable to him.

3. It stirred up her own gut and contributed to her tension headaches.

4. It disgusted some of her friends, who thought that Denny was much too nice to a "bitch" like her.

5. It was highly imperfect behavior for a would-be perfectionist like herself.

6. It consisted of indulgence in obsessive-compulsive behavior.

7. It sabotaged much of the joy in her life.

Flora gradually saw all these disadvantages of her compulsive public reproaches of Denny, but the one that mattered most to her was Denny finding her less lovable because of it. He was the first man who could almost completely accept her with her perfectionism, and she knew that if she lost him, she might well not find another accepting intimate relationship. She had to change her style if she wanted to remain with Denny.

For a while, Flora went to real extremes to be a "perfect non-perfectionist," backing off her criticism of Denny and even becoming careless and too forgiving. But she kept repeating her REBT homework to herself, very forcefully: "Denny has the right to be wrong, because he's a fallible human! All humans have the right to be wrong. That is their nature! Yes, me too. I'm not an idiot for keeping after Denny as I have been doing. But I act very idiotically. I'd better learn from my own mistakes. I don't have to. But I'd damned well better!"

Within several weeks, Flora gave both Denny and herself the right to be wrong. She also taught this right to her mother, sister, and two of her women friends. Her teaching them made it easier to apply it to herself. Later on, their friends began to comment that Flora and Denny were perhaps the most tolerant, forgiving couple they knew.

Pride in Being Right May Be a Mistake

Have you ever met anyone who was *never* wrong? Who *never* made a mistake? Have you *always* been right? Have you *never* made a serious error? Are you ready to acknowledge your mistakes? Or, do you pride yourself on being *always* right? Do you think that you are above making the mistakes your partner makes, "I would *never* do that!"

We've never met anyone who has never been wrong, or who never made a mistake. Yes, we ourselves have not always been right. We have made mistakes, and still make them.

Ted, however, was frequently unwilling to acknowledge his mistakes, and usually presented an outward picture of (almost) always being right:

I could and did rationalize creatively to maintain my image. (I still work on myself to acknowledge a mistake I've made, and to accept the consequences of that mistake.) I prided myself on being more mature and better than my first wife because I didn't do the immature things that she did. Then one day I read that people are usually on approximately the "same" emotional level of maturity (or immaturity) as those they marry. This was an interesting and challenging assumption for me. That evening, while lying in bed, I explored this notion as it might apply to me. "Does this mean that I'm on her emotional level?" I asked myself in horror. The idea was so repulsive to me that I immediately answered, "I can't be on that level of immaturity! I don't do what she does." But I was also aware that I had some emotional immaturity. "Could my emotional immaturity be on her level even if I expressed it differently?" I again asked myself.

I wrestled with this question all night, hardly getting any sleep. By the time morning came, I finally reluctantly accepted and acknowledged to myself, "Yes, I am on her level of emotional immaturity." And, "Although I don't do what she does, I do the equivalent in my own different way. I am neither more mature nor better, overall, than she is. But, I do have some maturity that she doesn't have, and she has some maturity I don't have." If we were open enough to the other's maturity, we could learn from each other, I thought. And, to some extent that is exactly what we did, we somehow did manage to learn from each other.

Unfortunately, emotional immaturity or disturbance is often characterized by resistance to learn from the maturity of others. By that morning, I concluded that my wife and I had emotional maturity and/also emotional immaturity. And/also! In this way I reconciled myself to my wife's immaturity and stopped seeing her as totally wrong for making mistakes. I gave both of us the right to be wrong. I was also "down there" on her level. I acquired more humility and lost some, but not all, of my emotional need to prove that I'm better or superior to others. In this way I also freed myself to more willingly and readily admit my mistakes and to allow others to make theirs. Since then I've learned the same lesson in a variety of other ways. [TC]

You Have a Right to Be Wrong

Shakespeare put it concisely: "To err is human." We word it a little differently in Guideline #6.

Give your partner the right to be wrong. Respect both of your rights to be fallible humans — your inalienable right to make mistakes and to learn from your own experiences and errors. Don't honor only your right to be an error-prone human!

Why is the right to make mistakes inalienable? Answer: We're all born fallible humans. Making mistakes is humanly unavoidable. You do make them, don't you? If you do, you will make it much easier on yourself and others if you readily acknowledge that fact. Remember Ben Franklin's refrain, "But of course, I may be mistaken about this matter. What do you think?" When you think your partner has made a mistake, you might reword Franklin's thought, "You remind me of myself. I make mistakes. I may be wrong about my conclusion. What do you think?"

When your partner attacks you for being wrong, you can ask yourself the rhetorical question, "Can I give myself the right to be wrong?" And, of course, your can answer, "Yes, I do have the right to be wrong!" The most important point however, is to give both your partner and yourself the right to make mistakes. And when it comes to you, give yourself the right to acknowledge your mistakes, at least tentatively, "Perhaps I did make a mistake. Let's look more closely at the situation." If your partner then says, "No, I don't think you were mistaken," the two of you may have a possible difference to share.

Learn From Your Mistakes
Mistakes are a part of learning. They may tell you where your limits are. They provide information that you "need" to change your approach. As we word it in Guideline #6, you have the "right to learn from your own experiences and errors." And your partner has the same right to learn from his or her own experiences and errors. You may choose to explore what your partner has learned from some mistake he or she acknowledges. If your experience is similar to Ted's, you may feel aghast at how superficial your partner's learning seems to be. However, this situation may be another opportunity to share and explore differences instead of telling your partner what she should have learned.

Elena was having some REBT sessions with Al to see how she could get over her anger at her business partner, Nora, who talked endlessly about what they could do to make the business better — instead working hard to actually improve it. Elena tried, according to REBT principles, to stop blaming Nora for her "laziness," to get Nora to admit that she would rather talk than do unpleasant business tasks, and to refuse to damn herself for her mistakes but instead to learn from them. Elena was frustrated by the weak response: Nora acknowledged some of her "laziness," made some poor excuses for procrastinating about making business deals, and made a minimal attempt to schedule her time at work a little more efficiently. She did not make the significant changes Elena expected, such as coming early and staying later at work, or stopping her procrastination on the calls she was to make.

Elena was angry at Nora's superficial and almost useless "learning." However, she remembered the REBT homily, "People have the right to be wrong, the right to blamelessly acknowledge their errors, and the right to not learn from their errors." She gave Nora these rights and reduced her anger. Then she went to sharing and exploring her differences with Nora about doing almost all business tasks immediately rather than procrastinating. Because Elena was no longer angry at her, Nora was able to listen, to share their difference, to agree on working longer hours if Elena also agreed to stop continually monitoring her, and to procrastinate less on making the business calls.

It's helpful to apply Guideline #1 as you work at accepting your and your partner's resistance to learning: "Allow yourself to *influence* your partner, but do not *demand* that he or she *must* change. Also, give her or him the freedom to influence you."

Learning usually works better when it comes as a self-discovery from the inside rather than suggested from the outside. It is usually better to share your differences and explore your disagreements rather than to impose your standards or beliefs on your partner.

Unfortunately, like so many people, you or your partner may repeat your mistakes rather than learn from them. "I frequently seem to require repeating a mistake several times," observes Ted, "before I emotionally realize that my mistake has something to teach me that it would be well for me to learn. I make my mistake in the pursuit of the goals I want to reach."

Jolanta discovered Guideline #6 when her boss at the health clinic where she worked closely questioned her about allowing me to go to Mexico for an alternate treatment for prostate cancer. He strenuously objected to any other approach than the traditional medical treatments. I had reasons of my own for objecting to some of the traditional medical treatments for prostate cancer. Jolanta objected to my choice also, but supported me in making my decision. As a physician, her boss thought that was a horrendous mistake and adamantly demanded that Jolanta should not, must not have allowed me to make it. She told him, "I can't do that to Ted because ... ." He angrily interrupted her, refusing to listen to her side, and got louder and more upset.

The more adamant her boss became, the more resistant Jolanta felt inwardly. Her inner resistance reminded her that I had allowed her to make her own mistakes, something that her own family almost never did, something that she valued in her marriage, and in her discoveries of herself. So she chose to support my right to make and learn from my mistakes. She let her boss blow off steam, decided to quit this job, and came home excited by her discovery of Guideline #6. Incidentally, her boss has been married three times, and apparently still hasn't learned how his demanding ways have contributed to spoiling his marriages. [TC]

(Ted was not cured of prostate cancer, but did learn how to keep this cancer under control.)

Guideline #6 Supports Integrity

One of the goals of Guideline #6 is to support the integrity of both partners. Our wording for part of this Guideline, "Don't honor only *your* right to be an error-prone human!" Support your partner's integrity and her or his "right" to live without the burden of your shoulds and musts.

If our theory is valid, you're born and reared with the tendency to have absolutistic shoulds and musts. They are part of our human condition. Our intention is to help you to become more aware of their dysfunctional potential, to acknowledge them, to learn to take then into account, compensate for them, and develop habits that reframe them. Your shoulds, musts, and demands can be converted into more useful, rational evaluations. Substituting, "It would be better if ...," for your shoulds, musts, and demands is a simple and "easy" starting point for such reframing. But we would be truly surprised if you succeeded in absolutely eliminating all of your dogmatic shoulds and musts, and — especially — your implied, unstated demands.

What assumptions do you have about mistakes? A common mistaken assumption is that the mistake powerfully determines what the consequences necessarily must be. Here again we mostly agree with famed family therapist Virginia Satir, "…that the event does not determine how to respond to the event. That is purely a personal matter. The way in which we respond will direct and influence the event more than the event itself." Believing that the event "dictates" how you respond to it, without any choice on your part, is itself often a serious mistake.

Also, when you wish that the event had never happened, you'll tend to use shoulds and musts. You probably tell yourself, "The event should not have happened," or, "It should have happened in some other way than it did." The fact of its happening may be acknowledged but then the "same" fact is rejected because it is so awful that it should not, *must not*, have happened. You mistakenly replace grim facts with your demand that they not exist.

Pauline was a client of Al's who had a large number of useless *shoulds* and *musts* about past, present, and future events. Particularly, that she should not have married Walt, who was (she thought) very nice but also very ugly. She should have known that his looks would interfere with their sex life. She should have realized that his being nice to her would get boring. She should have seen that he never would push himself very hard at his law practice. She should have predicted that their daughter, Jo, would love him more than her. Et cetera! Actually, Pauline was very bright and talented, she had an M.D., a Ph.D. and a Master's degree in public health. Therefore, she thought, a bright woman such as she should have been able to see, from the start, that Walt was not the husband for her and should have waited for a better candidate, although she was 35 — "almost over the hill" — when she met Walt.

When Pauline learned, in REBT sessions with Al, that very bright people have the right to act stupidly, she began to reduce her severe self-castigation. She also learned that you can't really predict what will happen in a relationship five years after marriage, that the other potential husbands could have turned out to be much worse than Walt, that she was exaggerating his "ugliness" by over focusing on it, and that her marriage actually had many advantages and lacked few "essentials." After several REBT sessions, Pauline stopped putting herself down for her "awful" stupidity, and relaxed into a very comfortable, though not ecstatic, marriage with Walt.

Blaming Can Start a Downward Cycle to Self-Pity

When you evaluate "bad" events with shoulds and musts, your tendency is to blame others, or to put yourself "one-down" as a victim of the event. This way, you can start an avoidable vicious downward cycle of emotional pain, depression, rage, or violence.

Abe and Fay saw Al for marital therapy. They had a pretty good marriage for seven years until Abe went bankrupt in his jewelry business and Fay lost her teaching job. Then the blaming began to fly — and fly! Abe damned himself for stupidly entering the jewelry business (at his father's urging), instead of becoming a well-paid accountant or lawyer, as he *should* have become. Fay looked down on him for not devoting himself thoroughly to his business as he *absolutely should* have done, and for not selling it before it went bankrupt, as he *should* have predicted it would. Fay downed herself for becoming a teacher instead of going through the harder work of being a dentist as she *could* have and definitely *should* have arranged to do, and for insisting on expensively furnishing their apartment instead of saving their wedding money and her earnings for a rainy day. Because she didn't save as she *should*, she and Abe had no funds to help him save his jewelry business or set up another one. Abe angrily criticized Fay because she wasn't willing to take a nonteaching job, any job, as she *should* have been to help them get by financially.

Abe and Fay's preoccupation with demeaning themselves and each other was wrecking their relationship. With their incessant *shoulding*, they gave each other no right to be wrong and consequently despised each other; they hated themselves as well as their behaviors. What's more, each thought that the other had no right to "unfairly" criticize, even though they viciously did so themselves. That produced more hatred. Their brutal accusations and blaming had some factual correctness, of course, for they both had human failings — a fact that Fay called to Abe's attention regularly and Abe "beat Fay over the head with." So they increased their other-hatred and self-hatred.

What a mess! It took several months of intensive REBT work to help Abe first, and a little more time afterward to help Fay, to forego their shoulding and musting on themselves and each other.

I first convinced Abe that Fay definitely had the right to be wrong. Seeing that, he could accept his own right to be fallible. Then I helped convince Fay that, she, too, could use this human right to be wrong by taking it herself and by giving it to Abe. Ah, success at last! Their finances continued to be poor for some time to come, but their relationship improved immensely. [AE]

You can stop wallowing in self-pity. You can stop confusing your shoulds, musts, and demands with *the absolute truth,* with the way "reality" should be (and therefore is). You can allow your partner the right to make the same mistakes you do, not for any other special reason, but just because, like you, your partner is human too.

Share Your Mistakes

Jolanta and Ted usually share their mistakes with each other.

We are discovering that we make many more mistakes than we thought we did before we started sharing them. Now for us, sharing mistakes is often enjoyable, is sometimes funny, does occasionally provide insight, but best of all, helps both of us to accept ourselves and each other "as is" more readily. In short, sharing our mistakes is a source of valuable bonding between us. We discover we are more alike than we had imagined ourselves to be. We are still learning that mistakes can be a valuable asset — even when they may also be a liability — "and/also" again. [TC]

What to do if mistakes — yours and/or your partner's — are still a serious disturbance in your relationship? We look at that problem in the next chapter.

11

Guideline 7:
Reconsider Your Wants as Goals

Reconsider your wants as goals that you may achieve later. When you don't get what you want or desire, remind yourself that you don't have to get what you want, now or ever!

Sometimes when you persistently use one or more of the Seven Guidelines, nothing seems to change; then you may feel discouraged. Ted did feel discouraged with Jolanta because, while he felt clear that he was using Guideline #1 with her, he didn't seem to have any impact on his wife.

We had developed and agreed on these guidelines together, so why wasn't she using Guideline #1? I concluded — mistakenly, it turned out — that she wasn't practicing it with me! But then I reminded myself that these Guidelines are a unilateral commitment, I had committed myself to use them no matter what she did and so continued practicing accepting her "as is." About a year later I noticed a change in her behavior. Instead of being grouchy, she was more pleasant when she got up in the morning and nicer toward me during the day.

Curious about this apparent change for the better, I shared my impression with her. She confirmed the change. It was then I learned that she had been quietly practicing accepting me "as is" all this time. I was surprised that it took me a year to notice it. Her change had been so gradual I had missed it. I gained a new appreciation for her persistence in working against her resistance. [TC]

Keep in mind that, unknown to you, your partner may be working on what you object to in her or him in a different way. Persist with your own commitment to accept your partner her or his way "as is" as the better way for you to go. There may be times when this is a difficult road to travel. If the difficulty persists, look for a pattern that repeats.

Look For a Pattern That Repeats

Take a look at the sidebar, "Outline of the Revolving Discussion Sequence — RDS," on this page. This easy-to-use communication tool was developed more than thirty years ago, and has helped thousands of couples and others to understand each other better.

Melva and Tom agreed to use Revolving Discussion Sequence (RDS) with each other: to listen carefully to each other, and to feed back their understanding of what each other said. Tom at first accused Melva of not listening to him, because she failed to repeat back his criticism that she talked too much when they conversed. Note that Tom and Melva experienced an incomplete RDS, leaving out the "checking back" procedure in the Understanding steps and leaving out the "Agreement" step entirely. Please review the sidebar. [TC]

Actually, Melva failed to repeat what Tom had said to her because she took what he said very seriously, accepted him "as is" with his "unfair" criticism, and immediately (wrongly) shut up. She told herself, "Even though I think he's wrong about my talking too much, I won't make myself angry at him, and won't break the RDS rule by arguing with him. I must immediately *show* him that I don't always speak too much. So I'll shut up and listen more *right now.*"

As they discussed why she didn't follow the RDS rule and repeat back Tom's accusation, Melva realized her self-demand, that she *must* immediately contradict him in *action.* Verbal feedback to him was not enough for her.

Outline of the Revolving Discussion Sequence — RDS

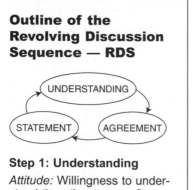

Step 1: Understanding

Attitude: Willingness to understand the other person *first.*

Intention: To understand the other person's issue the way she or he means it.

Procedure: (a) Without agreement or disagreement, state your understanding of the other's feeling, content, and meaning. (b) Check your understanding for fit: "Is that what you meant?" (c) Allow the sender to correct you. The sender, not you, is the authority of how well you understood. This protects the integrity of the sender. (d) Try again until the sender says, "You got it."

Tom decided to change his *demands* — that Melva listen more closely to him and not interrupt him with her constant talking — into a *strong preference.* He also started to redefine his *want* for her to talk less as a *goal* to be worked for and achieved in the future. He didn't *need* for her to "shut up right now," and he actually told her that he was working on giving up that need. He looked forward to mildly and politely indicating to her the times when her talking was "too much," forced himself to do just that and saw that his want was increasingly fulfilled. His redefined goal, no longer an immediate demand, made him actually look forward to gently — without anger — pointing out to Melva when she was talking too much.

Using REBT, Al helped Tom and Melva to arrive at a very similar place they would likely have attained if they had fully used RDS. These clients demonstrated the value of the RDS rules *by not fully using them.* Melva did not check back with Tom to make sure she understood him accurately. Nor did Tom ask her to check back with him. Their use of the RDS Understanding Step was incomplete. In effect, they *tried* using RDS without much success. Had they fully used the RDS Understanding Step, Melva would have first (a) restated Tom, as she did do, and second (b) checked for fit by asking Tom, "Is that what you are getting at?" Tom would have (c) corrected her immediately, and Melva would have (d) included that correction in her second try. When it became

---

Step 2: Agreement

Attitude: Desire to honestly share your agreement with the sender.

Intention: To expand your common ground.

Procedure: (a) Confirm some aspects of the other's position as valid. (b) Share honest agreements only; no disagreements yet. You are the authority on what you agree with. This protects your integrity. (c) Maximize your agreements. (d) Reverse roles and follow the sequence again.

Step 3: Statement

Attitude: Desire to move the dialogue toward a win-win.

Intention: To assist the listener in understanding your feeling, content, and meaning.

Procedure: (a) Present only *one* issue, clearly and briefly. Include your feelings. (b) If you disagree, state your difference with the other's position.

Continue the RDS sequence for one to three rounds, as desired.

Melva's turn to be understood by Tom, she could have explained her side of why she shut up. Their difficulty could have been handled sooner with less stress on both of them. Before using shortcuts it works better to get clear on the formal RDS procedures.[TC]

A Thirteen-Year Power Struggle

Louis and Ted have endured a *power struggle* for the last thirteen years and have made slow and slight progress in bettering the situation. A power struggle is a kind of contest, or game people play, over whose rules will govern the relationship. (Shoulds, musts, demands, or requirements are rules.) You cannot avoid a power struggle, but you can significantly improve your ground rules for communicating and relating to the other.

Louis and I are in the same group, helping to assist other groups with their communication difficulties. But, seemingly, we cannot handle our own communication difficulties. Jolanta asked Ted, "Why do you continue? It's a waste of your time. It is like repeatedly hitting the proverbial brick wall with your head."

I answered, "You make a good point. However, there is something I'm missing in my understanding of human communication that I have yet to learn. If I persist, I expect to learn what that missing part is." While I was writing this chapter, in our fourteenth year, Louis and I made a major breakthrough in our difficulty in communication.

The Breakthrough. Our difficulty was over whose issue was to be handled. Louis's issue was for us as a group to experimentally try out a "new" communication approach with other people who are not members of our group. And then to learn from our outreach.

My issue was, "That sounds good, but we often don't learn from our experience because we repeat our mistakes. Our major mistake is that we don't practice on ourselves what we try to teach others. Therefore let's work out the bugs within our group before trying to teach a new approach to others."

What is our fantasy here and what is the reality? In our power struggle we both had the fantasy that *repeating* our issues for how our group should and must behave will eventually convince the other of the *rightness* of our own issue, in spite of the reality of our 13-year history to the contrary.

Our breakthrough occurred when we discovered another previously unstated fantasy: that we would "save time by getting down to *the issue*." The phrase "the issue" implies there is only *one* issue. But our reality was that we have *two* issues: Louis's issue and Ted's issue.

What we did with this discovery was to choose to separate our two issues and take up each issue one at a time. This change in our rules worked beautifully for both of us. We handled in two hours what we wrestled with for thirteen years! Our power struggle had been over whose issue are we going to get down to.

Louis took this experience home to share with his wife. I experienced our discovery as of "cosmic" significance to be applied universally in all human communication.

I have had this cosmic experience before in other discoveries about human nature or human communication. And in no previous such experience has that great expectation been true. I didn't expect it to be true this time either. But for the moment it was an intoxicating fantasy which I thoroughly enjoyed. I immediately tried the same approach with my wife, Jolanta, to some good effect. What I learned with Louis was that, if I persist, eventually I will learn an important reality about communication that I hadn't fully appreciated before. [TC]

Fantasy in itself can sometimes be both fun as well as helpful. However, confusing fantasy with reality — as people often do with their use of shoulds, musts and demands — often makes simple problems more complex and difficult than is necessary. Shoulding and musturbation can even make some unwanted problems impossible to resolve.

Remember Frances and Frank a few chapters back? Frances's mother, Rose, strongly objected to her son-in-law. She wanted to protect her daughter from Frank's abusive attitudes and behavior by insisting that Frances must leave Frank. She provided Frances with a secret fund that Frances could use anytime she chose to leave Frank. But when Frances did not do what her mother thought was the right thing for Frances, Rose got emotionally highly upset and remained emotionally disturbed for several years. In this context Rose came to Ted and agreed to experimentally try a procedure he devised: a series of five questions, as described in the following section.

From Fantasy to Reality

The following exercise consists of five key questions you may ask yourself — or another — in order to explore the reality of a situation, and contrast that with your fantasy wish for how things might be "better." You may find it helpful as you work toward changing your *wants* into *goals*.

• The *set-up* questions:

1. *What do you specifically object to?* What's wrong with things as they are?

2. *What is the way you think it preferably* should *be?* Describe the situation if it were ideal — just the way you want it to be.

• The *transition* question:

3. *Why must it be the way you think it should be?* (*Shoulds* and *musts* exist in the world of fantasy.)

If you answered the third question with something like, "Because then things would be better" you have an unstated *should* or *must* in your thinking that your partner may be reacting to. You did not answer the transition question, "Must life be the way you think it should be." You answered a different question, "How do you prefer things to be?"

Try again. *"Why* must *the universe, God, life, people, things, or your partner conform to your demand?"* In your thinking, distinguish between (1) your desire or preference and (2) the compulsive demands of *shoulds* or *musts*.

• The *follow-through* questions:

4. *What is the actual "factual" reality?* Describe the way "it is," without judgmental words.

5. *What do you choose to do about what you object to?* If you can, list three possibilities to choose from. (If you wish, consider your fantasy as a goal to aim for. Change your compulsive shoulds and musts to "it would be better if" reality were the way I would like it to be, but remember *reality is the way "it is"!*)

Now let's apply these questions to Rose's situation:

• The *set-up* questions.

Question 1: *What does Rose specifically object to?* **Answer:** Frank not keeping his promises to Rose, his mother-in-law, and his commitments to his marriage to Frances. He is a Jekyll-and-Hyde kind of person.

Question 2: *What is the way Rose thinks it should be?* **Answer:** Frank should be the kind, loving person he was when courting Frances. But since he has turned out to be Mr. Hyde, her daughter should and must leave the marriage.

• The *transition* question:

Question 3: *Why must it be the way you, Rose, think it should be?* **Answer:** Because that would get rid of "the bastard" and then she could have a good relationship with her daughter. This is where Rose's confusion about what to do comes from. This response is Rose's fantasy and does not answer the question. Most people respond from their fantasy without realizing the fantasy quality in what they think would be better. Ted allowed Rose's response without challenging it and went on to question 4.

• The *follow-through* questions:

Question 4: *What is the actual "factual" reality?* **Answer:** Rose had trouble with stating the factual realty without using judgmental words. The "factual" reality for her was that Frank was a Jekyll and Hyde and was dangerous to the well-being of her daughter. When we explored that together we found that the factual reality was Frank did not behave the way Rose wanted but her daughter did not choose to leave her marriage at that time. And Rose's good intention is to be supportive of her daughter. This made a context for distinguishing between the factual reality and Rose's fantasy. We did not deny that her fantasy might be better than the factual reality. But reality is what she has to deal with and that is easier to do when the factual reality is acknowledged and accepted.

Rose had never before looked at her wishes and wants as a fantasy. She played with and tested ideas for their fantasy qualities for a while. She seemed to find distinguishing between fantasy and reality meaningful and fascinating. We went back to the transition question #3: *Why must Frank and your daughter's marriage be the way you, Rose, think it should be?* He answer now was, "It is the way it is. There is no reason why things *should* and *must* be the way I would *like* them to be." We were now ready for the final follow-though question.

Question 5: *What do you choose to do about what you object to?* **Answer:** I don't want to continue putting my daughter in the middle of a power struggle between her husband and me. I do want to be supportive of Frances. I'll allow Frances to make her decisions about leaving or staying in her marriage, and I'll support her right to make the mistakes I think she makes. I can give Frances emotional support. My goal is for Frances to be happy."

In her response, Rose did not say what she might do about Frank, other than stopping her end of the power struggle over who is going to decide what is best for Frances. After going through this procedure, she said she felt much better and relieved. Rose later wrote Ted a brief letter, reporting changes in some of her behavior, her further exploration of fantasies, and her growing ability to change her unrealistic wants into goals.

We have been illustrating this distinction between the fantasy of shoulds, musts, or demands and reality in this and previous chapters, now let's take another look at the seventh Guideline. This Guideline enables you make the other six Guidelines work for you:

Guideline #7

Reconsider your wants as goals that you may achieve later. When you don't get what you want or desire, remind yourself that you don't have to get what you want, now or ever!

Now that we've seen how each of the Seven Guidelines works, let's consider the importance commitment makes to the Seven Guidelines. That's the topic of the next chapter.

12

Using Commitment to Accomplish Your Goals

C ommitment provides persistence in moving toward your goal. Here is our suggestion for your commitment as you work with these Seven Guidelines for a great relationship:

Choose to practice the Seven Guidelines as a unilateral commitment, regardless of what your partner does or doesn't do. Each time you do not succeed, look to discover a mistake you may have made. You also may have something significant to learn about your way of talking or listening.

We don't know anyone who is perfect in use of the Seven Guidelines, including ourselves. It takes commitment to overcome discouragement when things don't seem to "work" right. That is okay for commitment. But why unilateral commitment? Because it gets rid of your significant emotional dependency on your partner to come through for you. If you require that your partner must do "his or her share" in using the Seven Guidelines, you may use that as justification or your excuse for stopping also. Because neither of you will likely be perfect in doing the Seven Guidelines, each of you will have times when each will perceive the other as not supporting these Guidelines. Then it probably will make no difference as to who stopped using them first. When you stop using them, your partner will justify her or his stopping because you stopped. Unilateral commitment can carry you through such discouraging occasions. And unilateral commitment gets rid of each blaming the other for not doing their part. Such a commitment is one-sided and does not require fairness.

Ted frequently felt discouraged when he thought Jolanta was not using one or more of the Seven Guidelines.

Then I would remind myself of my unilateral commitment and choose to bridge back to her in a non-blaming way. In time Jolanta also chose to bridge back to me in a non-blaming way also. Our relationship healed, instead of becoming a vicious downward circle.

The Seven Guidelines for Great Relationships and Better Communication

1. Accept your partner "as is." Determine that you are in your relationship to enjoy yourself, not to try to fix, reform, or straighten out your partner. Be responsible for your own feelings. Allow yourself to *influence* your partner, but do not demand that he or she *must* change. Also, give her or him the freedom to influence you. Yes, to persuade *and* inform you.

2. Express appreciation frequently. Acknowledge your partner often for small things. Find, discover, or even create things you really value about your partner. Say them. Honesty is important here. Avoid the main relationship "killer" — frequent criticism of your partner.

3. Communicate from integrity. Be honest regarding beliefs and evidence that conflict with your own views of what is happening. When your partner is right, admit it. Be both honest and tactful. Allow different perceptions to exist. Agree to stop penalizing each other for your honesty as you now often may do. Agree that both of you will be honest and let the other "get away" with honesty.

My unilateral commitment served us well.

Here, it might do well to quote Thomas Edison, "Opportunity is missed by most people because it is dressed in overalls and looks like work." What I find is an endless sequence of opportunities that when accepted often become enjoyable. My marriage with Jolanta often is enjoyable as well as my adventure in learning to create the life I really want to live. An adventure usually includes handling events that I don't want or that at first don't go right. That contrast between events I like and events I don't want make the journey an adventure. In effect, I make the journey my goal.

But if the journey is my goal what direction do I want to go? What then is my ultimate goal? [TC]

A Working Relationship

Roger Fisher stated it best in his book *Getting Together: Building Relationship as We Negotiate* (sequel to his bestselling *Getting to Yes*). **Pursue a "working" relationship.** At the outset, we need to clarify what we mean by a "good" relationship. What each of us wants from a relationship varies greatly. But whether I hope through my relationship with you to gain love, money, security, or something else, we are bound to face conflicting interests, perceptions, and values. Differences are bound to arise. And we will not get what we want unless we can handle those differences. In each of our relationships, whether between individuals, businesses, religious groups, or governments, we should seek to establish and maintain those qualities that will make it a good "working" relationship —one that is able to deal well with differences. [Fisher, 1988)

We agree that differences are bound to arise, and that a good "working" relationship is one that is able to deal well with differences. We see our Seven Guidelines as the next step — a way to develop the qualities necessary for a good — no, a *great* — relationship. To accomplish a truly great relationship takes *one-sided commitment*.

We encourage you to practice the Seven Guidelines as a unilateral commitment, regardless of what your partner does or doesn't do. Each time you have not succeeded, look to discover a mistake you may have made. You also may have something significant to learn about your way of talking or listening.

4. Share and explore differences with your partner. Explore disagreements with your partner to move toward a higher resolution that accepts parts of both your views. Or, to agree to disagree. Additionally, be ready to compromise without pretending that you agree when you really don't agree.

5. Support your partner's goals. Don't surrender your own integrity and your own important desires and views, but go as far as you honestly can to support your partner even when you clearly disagree.

6. Give your partner the right to be wrong. Respect *both* of your rights to be fallible humans — your inalienable right to make mistakes and to learn from your own experiences and errors. Don't honor only *your* own right to be an error-prone human!

7. Reconsider your wants as goals that you may achieve later. When you don't get what you want or desire, remind yourself that you don't *have* to get what you want, now or ever!

Let's see how that commitment works with each of the Seven Guidelines.

The Seven Guidelines are presented again on these two pages for easy reference. Here again is the "shorthand" version we've used in the following discussion:

Guideline 1: *Accept your partner "as is."*

Guideline 2: *Express appreciation frequently. Avoid steady criticism.*

Guideline 3: *Communicate from integrity.*

Guideline 4: *Share and explore differences with your partner.*

Guideline 5: *Support your partner's goals.*

Guideline 6: *Give your partner the right to be wrong.*
Guideline 7: *Reconsider your wants as goals.*

Guideline 1: Accept your partner "as is."

Accepting another "as is" mostly depends on your communication with yourself. Here's Ted's view:

Jolanta would work on herself to accept me "as is" each time she felt upset with me. Over time she got much better at reducing the length of time from a week to perhaps just an hour when she felt upset. Also the frequency of her upsets diminished. This was much better to live with, but I felt a little uneasy with the possibility of a sudden upset at almost anytime. Recently things have changed for the better again. Jolanta decided to fully accept me "as is" in principle. I no longer have that usual uneasy feeling. With this change our relationship has become more pleasurable for both of us.

Before revising this chapter, I visited with Jodean and Saundy with their permission to see how they were doing. Both were in an early Differences Group I moderated. And both were exposed to the early birth and growth of the Seven Guidelines. At that time Joe was ambivalent about marrying Saundy, but finally decided he wanted marriage when Saundy got interested in another man. I gave Joe the help he wanted to succeed with Saundy and he did marry her. Immediately after their wedding he privately told me he married the wrong woman. Later he decided it was my fault that he married Saundy.

While in this fame of mind he made marriage extremely difficulty for Saundy who went through a kind of hell seeking to please him. He was especially concerned about losing all his retirement money to Saundy's ways of managing money. She signed legal documents to safeguard his investments and money. But that was not enough for Joe's sense of emotional security. Nothing seemed to be good enough for him. Saundy has both strong, disciplined determination in general and commitment to her marriage with Joe. She experimented with every approach she could think of and find in books. Nothing seemed to work. Finally, she gave up trying to save their marriage and decided to let Joe call the shots. If he chose to leave the marriage she would support that. If he chose to stay in their marriage she would support that also. So now Joe was confronted by his own ambivalence.

Note: when Saundy fully accepted Jodean's ambivalence "as is" she also let go of her underneath demand that she must save her marriage. As it turned out this combination of acceptance and letting go of saving her marriage, saved the marriage. As Joe worked his way through his confusions he decided to risk his money with Saundy while she was getting her Ph.D. in Education by financially supporting her and emotionally support their marriage. Years later Joe phoned me to thank me for my role in his marrying such a wonderful person as Saundy. Joe is very open and not embarrassed about telling others that if it weren't for me they would not have married. Nor about telling them that later he cursed me, and now he is grateful to me. He loves Saundy. Her persistence and commitment finally paid off for both of them. [TC]

Ted, in this and other chapters of the book, has shown how he uses the *Seven Guidelines for Great Relationships and Better Communication* with his wife, Jolanta, and with several of his friends and colleagues. Al has shown how he teaches the *Guidelines* to his REBT clients and gives a good many examples of how this teaching works for them.

In this chapter, Al will expand on his use of the *Guidelines* by illustrating important aspects of his personal life with his partner, Janet Wolfe, and with some of his intimate associates. Here is his view on how he and Janet handled Guideline 1, *Accept your partner "as is."*

Janet and I have lived successfully with each other for 36 years, mainly because we accept each other "as is." We have many goals and interests in common — especially the goals of directing the Albert Ellis Institute in New York and its training affiliates in England, Europe, Asia, Australia, Mexico, and Canada. But in other interests and goals we often differ! Thus, Janet is interested in European and Asian art and has filled our apartment with antiques, paintings, photographs, and other exotic objects. I mildly enjoy the décor, but could easily live without it. My tastes are for modern furniture and my office (where I spend much of my time) is filled with practical, modern items. Janet reads large amounts of classical fiction in her leisure time, and I am devoted almost compulsively to reading nonfiction and to writing. Janet goes out, alone or with friends, to dinners, shows, operas, movies, parties, and other affairs; I do so perhaps once a year. When I am not traveling to give talks and workshops, I am a stay-at-home. Janet, although she can fulfill many happy and productive hours alone, is far more sociable than I. In these and many more ways, we are very different people. Yet, although we often disagree about many aspects of our lives, we rarely argue, fight, or blame each other for disagreeing. Why? Because we have taught ourselves, beginning in 1965 when we started living together, to fully accept each other "as is" — with all our warts, errors, and differences. Not that we *like* each other's tastes and distastes. Hardly! But we gracefully and tactfully accept them. Pretty damned steadily! So we remain happily — though not always ecstatically — and lovingly together. [AE]

Guideline 2: Express appreciation frequently.

This usually is easier to do when you accept your partner "as is." Now Mike and Liz are a mutual admiration couple as a team. It wasn't always that way. Mike remembered the steady criticism he got from Liz was her blaming him with such statements as "You always ..." and "You never ..." Liz loves to organize other people's lives, ways of doing business, or solving their problems. Mike resists being "organized" by Liz.

Liz concurs with Mike about her pre-Ted experience:

I looked at my upsets frequently mired in shoulds, musts and lots of have-to's. That was how I had lived my life ("You *should not* get pregnant before you get married, you *must* wear a dress when you go down town shopping, and you *have to* learn how to cook and keep house.") Mike was less willing to admit he had 'shoulds' or 'musts' and I was, I must say, particularly good (knee-jerk some would say) at defending my 'shoulds' or 'musts'. After all that was how the business world was able to get the work done, and that was the "membership dues," if you will, to become a revered society matron.

The other piece of our language that changed was absolutes: always, never, ever, everyone, everything — "You always..." Now *always* inspires us to say, "Always?" "Well almost always." Even when I use the absolutes, I stop and think to see if that's true and sometimes, well probably infrequently, it is.

"The beauty of living is pausing to reflect on some of the crazy things I said, wrote, did, or thought and rather than cringing, celebrating the changes and thanking those who were instrumental in pushing, prodding, challenging, or confronting me to grow. [Liz]

Mike's comment on the phone to Ted about Liz was, "Isn't she wonderful?" Liz is discovering what a gem she has for a husband. She seemed somewhat awe-struck because so many people tell her how much they like, or even love, Mike.

Al tells how he and Janet use Guideline 2: *Express appreciation frequently.*

> Janet excels me in this respect, because she often often expresses appreciation for my doings — both to me and to others. I can't say that I am as good as she is about this, since I become so busy and preoccupied that I fail to voluably appreciate the many things Janet does for me and for the Institute. Nevertheless, I think that I'm gradually getting a little better about following this Guideline. Janet is excellent at appreciating relatives, friends, and colleagues — yes, and even me! I am learning from her how to do this more!
>
> I am pretty good, however, at avoiding steady criticism. Not that I don't have a critical nature. I find scores of things "wrong" with Janet's, my friends', my clients', and my colleagues' behavior. But I almost always keep my big nasty trap shut, and I rarely tell Janet or other people off. Criticism, I recognize, frequently sabotages human relationships. So when I feel critical — which is fairly often — I stop myself from expressing my feelings, use REBT to vigorously question myself, feel sorry and disappointed about other people's *doings* but very rarely make myself angry at *them,* the human doers. Janet is more overtly honest and critical of people than I, but seldom maligns me. She often disagrees with my ways and points out my "errors." But she does so briefly and not intensely or prolongedly. [AE]

Guideline 3: Communicate from integrity

Coming from integrity is easier when you accept your partner "as is" and express honest appreciation to your partner. When coming from your integrity you may be wrestling with your own self-deception — a common human trait. Both couples — Saundy-Jodean and Mike-Liz — discovered some of their self-deceptions in their attitudes and ways of talking.

Liz wrote what she and Mike learned:

> Another important shift for both Mike and I has been the conviction that we can not change. (A self-deception because they could and did change.) Early in our marriage if I complained about Mike's

behavior his response was: "Well, that's just the way I am. I can't change." Learning our ABC's (*activating event, belief,* and *consequences*) opened up new possibilities for personal growth. Wow, if I can change my thoughts (B) or feelings about a potentially upsetting experience (A) I could have a changed experience (C).

Before REBT, both Mike and I believed that other people (and especially each other) could make us mad, glad, sad, bad, etc. When we realized what power we had given others for our own feelings, we took it back. I'm in charge of what I'm feeling (even if I'm having trouble at the moment figuring out what it is) and so is everyone else in charge of his/her own feelings. Mike will sometimes challenge others (never in business dealings, however) who say, 'You make/he made ..' 'I DID? HE DID? The speaker usually pauses and frequently corrects himself. [Liz]

Jodean reported that he learned from Ted to take responsibility for his feelings. His self-deception was that he was not responsible for his feeling. Like Liz and Mike, Joe thought other people *caused* him to feel what he felt. Self-honesty required correcting their self-deception.

Al noted the following about Guideline 3: *Communicate from integrity.*

I think that I can honestly say that Janet and I seldom lie to ourselves or to each other about our feelings. When Janet thinks I am too pontificating or arrogant about preaching the virtues of REBT, she doesn't equivocate or tone down her comments, but frankly tells me her view. I may at first disagree with her, but I look into my heart and usually see that she has some good points. I then accept *myself* "as is," but am critical of my *behavior* and resolve to change it. Not that I always do! But at least I try to keep reminding myself that I'd better change. When I honestly think that Janet is wrong — for example, about making and implementing an important policy in her capacity as Executive Director of our Institute — I risk telling her my opinion, but in a nonblaming manner. So we both keep our integrity, even when we seriously disagree. [AE]

Guideline 4: Share and explore differences with your partner.

Achieving a win/win becomes realistically possible when you accept your partner "as is," share and explore disagreements, express appreciation frequently, and come from honest integrity. The "catch," or difficulty, here is in successfully sharing and exploring of disagreements. Disagreements are more often argued over, or avoided, than successfully shared. This guideline works better when you assume that your partner has a side worth considering.

What Ted does with that "catch" is to assume that there is something more for him to learn about communication and the successful sharing of differences or disagreements.

Liz put it this way:

When we got to RDS (Revolving Discussion Sequence) in our group I said, "I love it because it has rules!" (But don't for minute think that Mike and I didn't argue over who had the rules right.) The protocol appealed to me because I was assured that 1) I'd get my chance for my side of the story and 2) he'd have to find something about my position to agree with. At least I'd be right and he'd have to agree with me! It did mean, however, that I needed to do the same for Mike. I had been so good at token and grudging agreement before and since he was to be the authority over whether he felt heard or not I needed to start playing fair (rats!). [Liz]

Mike tackles the "catch" by asking Liz, "Do you want to be right or do you want to be understood?" Mike usually did a thoughtful job of understanding another, which is a rare gift. Good understanding from the receiver is almost always experienced by the sender as a loving gift.

Saundy learned from RDS that the message received usually is not the message sent. She tries to pinpoint the confusion between the sender and the receiver. If she fails to resolve the confusion she has a conversation with herself using five questions. For example:

1. What is the problem?
Jodean does not make a decision about our marriage. I'm left up in the air.
2. What do you want?
I want him to commit himself to making our marriage work.
3. What are you doing about it?
Complaining and crying.
4. Is it working?
No.

5. What are you willing to do now that might work?

To support Joe's decision either way he chooses and to refuse to try any more ways to save our marriage.

Jodean approached the "catch" by giving false agreement to Saundy, and then discovering 24 hours later that she was right.

In regard to using Guideline 4 — *share and explore differences with your partner* — Al reports:

Janet and I may not be the greatest partners in following Guideline 4. We often do our best to implement it, however.

A number of years ago, I seriously disagreed with Janet about what I thought was the overly-firm manner in which she was getting after one of our staff members. Vivian seemed to be quite lax in her duties, often promised to meet deadlines, then would forget about her promises. Faced with this behavior, I merely kept reminding her, once again, of her promises. Eventually, with some surliness, she would carry them out — at least some of them. So I partly got what I wanted from her. But Janet, with overall responsibility for insuring the functioning of the Institute, kept after Vivian, and often induced her to keep her promises more promptly.

I was afraid that Vivian would make herself very angry at Janet's pushing, and that she would quit before we could find someone to replace her. So at first I argued with Janet about this — to no avail. In fact, we verged upon getting into one our rare fights.

Sometime before this situation arose, Ted and I had worked together on the *Seven Guidelines*, so I decided to give more thought to Guideline 4. I asked myself whether there possibly was something I could do to achieve a win-win position in this disagreement with Janet. I finally figured out that there were *advantages to me* if Janet held to her firm position. Among them were: (1) I would save time by letting Janet deal with Vivian on some of the tasks we wanted her to complete; (2) Vivian might quit in a huff and the Institute would not have to pay unemployment insurance for her; (3) I would please Janet by going along for her ride, even though I thought she was handling the situation wrongly; (4) I would be much more motivating to Janet in handling her administrative responsibilities if I didn't bother her too much about how "badly" she was handling our problem employee; (5) Without my hassling opposition to Janet's way, she would be freer to handle other important problems that the Institute was trying to solve.

When I went out of my way to see the advantages for both me and Janet of letting her handle Vivian "badly," I easily let Janet have her way, tended to my own business, and saw more than ever the virtue of using Guideline 4 in our life together. I then shared some of my differences with Janet, told her I was willing to compromise my own position on this matter, let her proceed with setting goals and deadlines for our employees, and merrily went about my own way. As it happened, Vivian actually did quit and, after a period of some difficulty, the Institute replaced her with a much more responsive person. [AE]

Guideline 5: Support your partner's goals

When you accept your partner "as is," express appreciation frequently, come from honest integrity, and are open to learning from each other in the successful sharing and exploring of differences and disagreements, supporting your partner's constructive goals and purposes becomes easy. Ted, as a non-Christian, chooses to support Jolanta's purpose to experience more of the love of God. Jolanta, contrary to her own view of what to do, chose to support Ted in trying an alternative treatment for his prostate cancer. Jodean chose to support Saundy by moving from Los Angeles to Bakersfield, and buying a new house for her so she could be near her work. Liz supported Mike's wish to risk salesmanship as a source of income. He became successful. Mike joined each class or workshop that Liz wanted to experience.

Guideline 5 — *Support your partner's goals* — worked for Al and Janet in the case of the problem of Institute staff member, Vivian, described above. Here are Al's observations:

My goal and purpose, in the difference Janet and I had about forcefully pushing Vivian to be more efficient, was at first to keep her working for us at all costs, since she eventually got around to the work she did for me and did it very well. Janet's goal was to firmly get after her until she stopped making excuses for her delinquencies and radically changed her ways for the better. If she didn't, Janet thought, we should definitely get rid of her because she was doing us more harm than good.

Because Janet and I held our opposing views, kept discussing them, and did so without any hostility toward each other, we shared and explored our differences thoroughly. We then got through some quite trying weeks with this problem employee, focused on solving the problems we had with her (instead of upsetting ourselves about them), and finally solved some of them. We did this by allowing each other the leeway of handling Vivian our own individual ways and accepting the fact that each of our own ways significantly differed from the other's. I benefited by learning how to be firmer with our other executives and Janet learned how to feel less upset with some of our other employees — at least with those who acknowledged their errors and strove to improve their performances. [AE]

Guideline 6: Give your partner the right to be wrong

Again, this is easy to do if you follow the previous guidelines with acceptance, appreciation, integrity, sharing of differences, and support of goals.

The writing of this book was a collaborative effort. Al and Ted and Bob Alberti (our editor) shared our differences without blaming each other for any of the many mistakes made in the writing. Usually Jodean and Saundy acknowledge their disagreements without blaming the other for being wrong. Mike and Liz enjoy sharing their mistakes with others as a source of innocent merriment.

Ted admits he sometimes has trouble giving Jolanta the right to make mistakes.

Typically I may have forgotten to accept her 'as is' (#1) and criticize Jolanta for not exploring a disagreement between us (#4), as she should of course. At that moment I have also forgotten to give her the right to make a mistake (#6). Sometimes I even get angry or upset. I make no claim to perfection. When I catch myself forgetting like this I seek some way to bridge back to her. [TC]

The Guidelines support each other.

Al dealt with what he considered Janet's "mistake" in being too forceful with the Institute's employee, "Vivian," by reminding himself:

Maybe *I'm* wrong in seeing Janet's pushing Vivian so hard as "wrong." Maybe Janet will succeed in her efforts. Even if I *am* right and Janet is wrong — about this or other "mistakes" that I believe she makes — nothing *terrible* or *awful* will happen. Only inconveniences! My fighting with Janet over her "mistakes" will probably distract her from correcting them, now and in the future. If she knows that I hate her "mistakes," but still accept *her* with them, that will help us to have a better relationship and enjoy the things we agree about. By accepting Janet with her "errors," I will upset myself less and will be able to do many more of the things I want to do in this all-too-short life I have. By not plaguing Janet about her "mistakes," I will give her more freedom to enjoy her chosen life and to have a partner who is happier for her doing so; she will then, probably, be more forgiving of me. If so, Janet will be happier herself, will allow me to make my common mistakes, will accept me no matter how "wrong" she thinks I am, and will have the leeway to be more productive.

Making myself think this way, instead of resenting the way Janet was thinking and acting about Vivian, I was granting Janet the right to be "wrong." This Guideline helped us get along even better. [AE]

Guideline 7: Reconsider your wants as goals
If you...

accept both your partner and yourself "as is" (#1), frequently appreciate both your partner and yourself (#2), support honest integrity in communicating for both your partner and yourself (#3), allow yourself to share what you don't want to hear from your partner and tactfully share what your partner does not want to hear from you (#4), at least partially support your partner's constructive goals and purposes (#5), openly allow everyone to make mistakes including yourself and allow everyone to acknowledge their mistakes without punishment (#6)...
then you likely will have little need for this Guideline.

Guideline #7 provides a graceful escape from your own compulsive or obsessive demands and gives you more flexibility to adjust to your immediate or long-range situation. It provides a direction for you to go. It allows you to continue to want what you desire while freeing yourself of being rigidly stuck within your position. It frees you of feeling depressed when your want is not immediately gratified. It focuses on long range hedonism and can make the pursuit of your goal a pleasure as well as a challenge to your innate creativity. In short, changing your want into a goal is truly a significant change of your attitude.

Saundy changed her want for marriage with Jodean into a goal: allowing him to solve his problem of ambivalence. She gave him the problem to solve when she refused to continue trying to solve it and decided to fully accept his choice.

When Jodean later chose to risk his retirement money to pay for Saundy's university education he changed his wanting and demanding a guarantee of financial security to the later possibility that their combined incomes will provide the security he wanted. Indeed, he even changed his wanting to provide for himself in favor of supporting and providing for Saundy and himself.

Liz changed her wanting to control and organize Mike's life to the goal of a marriage partnership with Mike that they both can contribute to. Mike changed his want to be himself into a goal of growing to be more maturely himself while supporting constructive changes in their marriage.

As you can see, changing your want into a goal yet to be achieved may also include changing what you want. It is a significant part of the process of maturing in the continuing challenge of living..

Al comments on Guideline 7 — *Reconsider your wants as goals* — this way:

My want or desire about Janet being less forceful with our staff member, "Vivian," at first was to induce her to push Vivian less, to be more patient with Vivian's deliberately slow work style, and to give us more time to replace Vivian. I gave up this want for the present and allowed Janet to continue her presumably overly-forceful way with Vivian. I accepted Janet "as is," and kept myself from fighting with her over our disagreement about how she should handle the situation; this allowed us unhostilely to share our disagreements. I gave Janet my support for her "wrong" management style, and everything finally worked out well.

I didn't give up my want, however, but made it a goal for the future. I kept wanting, in the future, to handle difficult employees patiently and unangrily, and to convince Janet to do likewise. But I didn't *need* to have my goal met, now or in the future. I kept my *goal* as a strong *preference*, and didn't demand that I or Janet implement it, so I had no impasse or active disagreement with Janet in connection with this goal. (But I *still* would like my goal to be fulfilled!) [AE]

We will borrow Liz's comment for ending this chapter:
When Ted introduced "framing" I had no idea how significant it would be for my world view. Through the years I have watched and listened to business leaders, politicians, church officials and followers, activists, cultural representatives and tried to figure out what their frame was. I saw and heard so many people "stuck" in their frame without the ability (or even the desire) to move to another's frame

('That is the way IT is and not just how I see it.') And that brings us back full circle to REBT. When you see (or read or hear) disconfirming data you better change or rethink or challenge or at least be honest with yourself about these beliefs. Otherwise, you're stuck. [Liz]

We will give you a simple, but not always easy, way to learn the Seven Guidelines in the next chapter.

13

Making The Seven Guidelines Work For You

T hroughout this book, we have emphasized the importance of following our Seven Guidelines for Great Relationships and Better Communication. We've given you lots of examples, and told you how to include Rational Emotive Behavior Therapy and Revolving Discussion Sequence into your application of the guidelines. In this final chapter, we want to give you some specific ideas for learning the Guidelines and making them an ongoing part of your relationship.

Tips for Learning and Using the Guidelines

To start you off, here are three simple tips:

Tip #1: *Learn "by littles."* Take one small bite size piece to "master" at a time. Don't overload youself by trying to learn these Seven Guidelines all at once.

Tip #2: *Test our assertions,* one at a time. Test our claims to prove to yourself that the Seven Guidelines are valid. Or to prove them false. Be willing to reword our guidelines to make them more understandable or workable for yourself.

Tip #3: *Make continuing small improvements* in your understanding or use of the Seven Guidelines every week. Aim for improvement, not for perfection. Persist!

From Ideas to Action

We don't expect you to take our word for it that the Seven Guidelines will change your life. What we really hope you'll do is try them out for yourself. Discover in your own life whether or not they work for you.

To help you find out, we've created an easy-to-follow review format. For each of the Seven Guidelines, you'll find a brief statement of purpose, a "key" for understanding and applying the guideline, specific action you can take to try out the Guideline, and space for you to jot down a couple of suggestions for applying the guideline in your life. We think you'll find the following steps a useful procedure for trying the Guidelines out for yourself.

Guideline #1: *Accept your partner "as is."*

Purpose: *To put you in charge of yourself* in a way that supports your partner's right to choose and to contribute to a self-correcting relationship with you. And to give you inner peace of mind.

Key: *Assume responsibility for your feelings.*

Suggestion: *Observe your own avoidance thinking* or refusal to accept reality. Challenge yourself to accept the adversities that may be "unacceptable" to you.

Choose your own self-suggestions:
1)
2)

Guideline #2: *Express appreciation frequently.*

Purpose: *Don't "judge."* Accept your partner as a loving, caring person. Help each other grow to your "fullest" potential. To support a happy relationship with your partner though honest emotional support and acknowledgment without the destructive effects of criticism.

Key: *Expressing frequent honest appreciation for small things* has an accumulative effect for making the communication environment "safe" for your partner to open up and share more honestly with you. Catch your partner doing something right. Share that something with your partner.

Suggestion: Everything has both advantages and disadvantages. "And/also." Look for and discover the advantage in what you object to.

Choose your own self-suggestions:
1)
2)

Guideline #3: *Communicate from integrity.*

Purpose: *To keep your relationship on a basis of trust,* keep yourself emotionally free of traps or entanglements that violate your integrity.

Key: *Honestly and readily acknowledge* (a) what is going on with your partner, (b) what is going on with yourself, and (c) what is going on in the relationship. Acknowledge what you feel and think. Acknowledge your weaknesses, your inconsistencies, and your unfulfilled promises. Acknowledge your strengths and what you like about yourself.

Suggestion: *Accept your fears that honesty and integrity will not always make you look good.* Honesty and integrity require courage to face your fears and to learn from your mistakes. Learn to time your honesty by saving your problem for the right occasions to share.

Choose your self-suggestions:
1)
2)

Guideline #4: *Share and explore differences with your partner.*

Purpose: *To establish cooperation* in the solving of social problems, conflict reduction, and to enjoy the pleasures of cooperative creativity.

Key: *Assume that your partner always has a position worth considering.* Listen for your partner's issue. If you're talking, you aren't listening.

Suggestion: *Look for and find something right,* useful, or true in your partner's position. Focus on understanding your partner's central issue as your partner sees it.

Choose your self-suggestions:
1)
2)

Guideline #5: *Support your partner's goals.*

Purpose: *To express your love for your partner* in practical and supportive ways.

Key: *Clarify what you choose to mean* by constructive "purposes," and by "integrity."

Suggestion: *Support your partner's right to develop the unique individual he or she is* as a separate person from yourself. See disagreements as differences and think of differences as resources that can enrich your relationship with your partner when differences are successfully shared.

Choose your self-suggestions:
1)
2)

Guideline #6: *Give your partner the right to be wrong.*

Purpose: *To affirm your partner's right to be imperfect* and a fallible human. Allow room and support for your partner to learn and grow into his or her own constructive potential.

Key: *Refuse to be embarrassed or ashamed* of your mistakes or your humanness. Acknowledge your similarities with your partner. You can bond on your similarities. You too are imperfect and a fallible human. You also have mistaken assumptions and make mistakes.

Suggestion: *Readily acknowledge your mistakes* and your forgetting to your partner — more or less when you discover them.

Choose your self-suggestions:
1)
2)

Guideline #7: *Reconsider your wants as goals.*

Purpose: *To release you from the demands of shoulds and musts* and the trap of "either/or" that you either *must* get what you want or you give in to the hopeless despair of *never* getting what you want.

Key: *Remind yourself frequently that you don't have to get what you want.* What you want is not guaranteed by God, chance, or nature. You may, or you may not, get it. You will discover what you get, or don't get, in time.

Suggestion: *Keep your wants, intentions, and desires as valid for you.* If you work to achieve a want, you may get it. But keep your want as a future goal you work for. When you let go of the *demand* to get what you want, you may also increase the probability of getting it.

Choose your self-suggestions:
1)
2)

Unilateral commitment: *Commmit yourself to follow the guidelines* even if your partner chooses not to do so. You are making a unilateral commitment to improve your relationship.

Purpose: *To avoid the almost-certain failure to achieve a mutual commitment* for using the Seven Guidelines.

Key: *You are 100% responsible for your own learning and use of the Seven Guidelines.* If there is a mutual commitment, each one makes a unilateral commitment of responsibility to learn and use the Seven Guidelines regardless of what the other does.

Suggestion: Make learning and using the Seven Guidelines your future goal yet to be achieved until your have "mastered" both understanding them and using them.

Choose your self-suggestions:

1)

2)

Choosing to listen may lead to confusion. If you are confused, you should be confused just because that is the way it is for you at the moment. Accept your confusion, then get more information or make an experimental arbitrary decision and see what happens.

Just A Little Afraid, Are You?

When using these Seven Guidelines, you likely have some unrecognized fear or viewpoint that blocks your learning. If you have fear, you have three basic choices. First is *to acknowledge that you choose to master your fear* "and/also" that to some significant extent you are already ruled by your fear. This seems true for most people. Try an "and/also" evaluation of your fear. Second is to *confront your fear.* Your third choice is to *let your fear rule you.* Which do you choose to be master, you or your fear? ("Either/or.") We hope you will choose to "master" your fear as a goal yet to fully achieve rather than be ruled by your fear. If you have no fear, and it is only your viewpoint that blocks your using the Seven Guidelines to help you improve your relationship, let the guidelines be a challenge for your own growth.

Forward From Here

Ultimately you choose how to deal with differences and disagreements in your life. We suggest that you make it a conscious choice, whether you choose our Seven Guidelines or create your own unique approach.

Recall our discussion of Guideline 6 in chapter 10. We are all fallible humans. You and your partner, regardless of your commitment, will not always succeed in following the Guidelines — or in any other aspect of your lives. When you fail to achieve your intended goals, first reassess; then, if you still desire to achieve the goal, persist. Remember that the road to Carnegie Hall is paved with *practice, practice, practice!*

We're confident that you'll find the Seven Guidelines a valuable tool for making your relationship great and your communication better, and we urge you to give them a try.

We wish you well.

Selected References

The following references include the works of some of the main authors mentioned in this book, but mainly include those authors who have dealt with self-help materials. Also included are a number of items on Rational Emotive Behavior Therapy (REBT) and Cognitive Behavior Therapy (CBT), which may be useful for self-help purposes. Many of the items in this list of references may be obtained from the Albert Ellis Institute, 45 East 65th Street, New York, NY 10021-6593. The Institute's free catalogue and other materials for distribution may be ordered by sending your mailing address on weekdays by phone at (212) 535-0822, by fax at (212) 249-3582, or e-mail at orders@rebt.org. The Institute will continue to make available these and other materials, and it will offer talks, workshops, and training sessions, as well as other presentations in the area of human growth and healthy living and will list these in its free regular catalogue.

Adler, A. (1964). *Social interest: A challenge to mankind.* New York: Capricorn.

Alberti, R., & Emmons, M. (1995). *Your perfect right.* 7th ed. Atascadero, CA: Impact Publishers.

Barlow, D. H., & Craske, N. G. (1994). *Mastery of your anxiety and panic.* Albany, NY: Graywind Publications.

Beck, A. T. (1988). *Love is not enough.* New York: Harper & Row.

Bernard, M. E. (1993). *Staying rational in an irrational world.* New York: Carol Publishing.

Broder, M. S. (1990). *The art of living.* New York: Avon.

Burns, D. D. (1980). *Feeling good: The new mood therapy.* New York: Morrow.

Burns, D. D. (1993). *Ten days to self-esteem.* New York: Morrow.

Covey, S. R. (1992). *The seven habits of highly effective people.* New York: Simon & Schuster.

Crawford, T., & Ellis, A. (1989). A dictionary of rational-emotive feelings and behaviors. *Journal of Rational-Emotive and Cognitive-Behavioral Therapy,* 7 (1), 3–27.

Csikszentmihaly, M. (1990). *Flow: The psychology of optimal experience.* San Francisco: Harper Perennial.

Dryden, W. (1999). *How to accept yourself.* London: Sheldon.

Dryden, W., & Gordon, J. (1991). *Think your way to happiness*. London: Sheldon Press.

Ellis, A. (1960). *The art and science of love*. New York: Lyle Stuart & Bantam.

Ellis, A. (1957/1975). *How to live with a neurotic: At home and at work*. New York: Crown. Rev. ed., Hollywood, CA: Wilshire Books, 1975.

Ellis, A. (1962). *Reason and emotion in psychotherapy*. Secaucus, NJ: Citadel.

Ellis, A. (1972/1991). *Psychotherapy and the value of a human being*. New York: Albert Ellis Institute for Rational-Emotive Therapy.

Ellis, A. (Speaker). *How to stubbornly refuse to be ashamed of anything*. Cassette recording. New York: Albert Ellis Institute.

Ellis, A. (1976). The biological basis of human irrationality. *Journal of Individual Psychology, 32*, 145–168. Reprinted. New York: Albert Ellis Institute.

Ellis, A. (Speaker). (1976b). *Conquering low frustration tolerance*. Cassette recording. New York: Albert Ellis Institute.

Ellis, A. (Speaker). (1977). *Conquering the dire need for love*. Cassette recording. New York: Albert Ellis Institute.

Ellis, A. (1988). *How to stubbornly refuse to make yourself miserable about anything—yes, anything!* Secaucus, NJ: Lyle Stuart.

Ellis, A. (1994). *Reason and emotion in psychotherapy*. Revised and updated. Secaucus, NJ: Carol Publishing Group.

Ellis, A. (1996a). *How to maintain and enhance your rational emotive behavior therapy gains*. Rev. ed. New York: Albert Ellis Institute.

Ellis, A. (1996b). *REBT diminishes much of the human ego*. Rev. ed. New York: Albert Ellis Institute.

Ellis, A. (2000). *How to control your anxiety before it controls you*. New York: Citadel.

Ellis, A. (1999). *How to make yourself happy and remarkably less disturbable*. Atascadero, CA: Impact Publishers.

Ellis, A., & Becker, I. (1982). *A guide to personal happiness*. North Hollywood, CA: Melvin Powers.

Ellis, A., & Blau. S. (1998). (Eds). *The Albert Ellis Reader*. Secaucus, NJ: Carol Publishing Group.

Ellis, A., & Harper, R. A. (1961/1997). *A guide to rational living*. North Hollywood, CA: Melvin Powers.

Ellis, A., & Harper, R. A. (1961). *A guide to successful marriage*. North Hollywood, CA: Wilshire Books.

Ellis, A., & Knaus, W. (1977). *Overcoming procrastination*. New York: New American Library.

Ellis, A., & Lange, A. (1994). *How to keep people from pushing your buttons*. New York: Carol Publishing Group.

Ellis, A., & MacLaren, C. (1998). *Rational emotive behavior therapy: A therapist's guide.* Atascadero, CA: Impact Publishers.

Ellis, A., & Tafrate, C. (1997). *How to control your anger before it controls you.* Secaucus, NJ: Birch Lane Press.

Ellis, A., & Velten, E. (1992). *When AA doesn't work for you: Rational steps for quitting alcohol.* New York: Barricade Books.

Ellis, A., & Velten, E. (1998). *Optimal aging: How to get over growing older.* Chicago: Open Court Publishing.

Fisher, R., Ury, W. & Patton, B. (1981). *Getting to yes.* Boston, MA: Houghton Mifflin Co.

Fisher, R. & Brown, S. (1988). *Getting together: Building relationships as we negotiate.*

FitzMaurice, K. E. (1997). *Attitude is all you need.* Omaha, NE: Palm Tree Publishers.

Frankl, V. (1959). *Man's search for meaning.* New York: Pocket Books.

Froggatt, W. (1993). *Rational self-analyses.* Melbourne: Harper & Collins.

Glasser, W. (1998). *Choice theory.* New York: Harper Perennial.

Glasser, W. (2000). *Reality therapy in action.* New York: Collins.

Haley, J. (1953). *Strategies of psychotherapies.* Grune and Stratten

Hauck, P. A. (1973). *Overcoming depression.* Philadelphia: Westminster.

Hauck, P. A. (1991). *Overcoming the rating game: Beyond self-love—beyond self-esteem.* Louisville, KY: Westminster/John Knox.

Hayakawa, S. I. (1941). *Language in action.* New York: Harcourt, Brace & Co.

Homey, K. (1950). *Neurosis and human growth.* New York: Norton.

Horvath, A. T. (1998). *Sex, drugs, gambling, and chocolate.* Atascadero, CA. Impact Publishers.

Kantor, N. *Employee counseling.*

Kelly, G. (1955). *The psychology of personal constructs.* New York: Norton.

Kirsch, I. (1999). *How expectations shape experience.* Washington, D.C.: American Psychological Association.

Korzybski, A. (1933/1990). *Science and sanity.* Concord, CA: International Society of General Semantics.

Lange, A., & Jakubowski, P. (1976). *Responsible assertive behavior.* Champaign, IL: Research Press.

Lazarus, A. A. (1985). *Marital Myths.* Atascadero, CA: Impact Publishers.

Lazarus, A. A. & Lazarus, C. N. (1997). *The 60-second shrink.* Atascadero, CA: Impact Publishers.

Mahoney, M. J. (1991). *Human change processes.* New York: Basic Books.

Maslow, A. H. (1954). *Motivation and personality.* New York: Harpers.

Maultsby, M. C., Jr. (1984). *Rational behavior therapy.* Englewood Cliffs, NJ: Prentice-Hall.

McMullin, R. E. (2000). *The new handbook of cognitive therapy.* New York: Norton.

Meichenbaum, D. (1977). *Cognitive-behavior modification.* New York: Plenum.

Miller, T. (1986). *The unfair advantage.* Manlius, NY: Horsesense, Inc.

Mills, D. (1993). *Overcoming self-esteem.* New York: Albert Ellis Institute.

Perls, F. (1969). *Gestalt therapy verbatim.* New York: Delta.

Phadke, K. M., & Chularii, V. (1997). *Conquering laziness.* New Delhi, India: Excel Books.

Pietsch, W. V. (1993). *The serenity prayer.* San Francisco: Harper San Francisco.

Rapoport, A. (1950). *Science and the goals of man.* New York: Harper & Bothers

Rogers, C. R. (1942). *Counseling and psychotherapy.* New York: Houghton Mifflin.

Rogers, C. R. (1961). *On becoming a person.* Boston: Houghton-Mifflin.

Russell, B. (1930/1985). *The conquest of happiness.* London: Unwind.

Satir, V. (1972). *Peoplemaking.* Science and Behavior Books.

Satir, V. (1983). *Conjoint family therapy.* Science and Behavior Books

Seligman, M. E. P. (1991). *Learned optimism.* New York: Knopf.

Seligman, M. E. P. (1995). The effectiveness of psychotherapy: *The Consumer Reports* study. *American Psychologist, 50,* 965–974.

Simon, J. L. (1993). *Good mood.* La Salle, IL: Open Court.

Taylor, S. E. (1990). *Positive illusions: Creative self-deception and the healthy mind.* New York: Basic Books.

Tillich, P. (1953). *The courage to be.* Cambridge: Harvard University Press.

Walen, S., DiGiuseppe, R., & Dryden, W. (1992). *A practitioner's guide to rational-emotive therapy.* New York: Oxford University Press.

Wolfe, J. L. (Speaker). (1980). *Woman—assert yourself.* Cassette recording. New York: Albert Ellis Institute.

Wolfe, J. L. (1992). *What to do when he has a headache.* New York: Hyperion.

Young, H. 5. (1974). *A rational counseling primer.* New York: Institute for Rational-Emotive Therapy.

Index

RebuildingBooks
For Divorce and Beyond™